WATER

Getting off

with 240+ visual aids

Aquatics Unlimited, Inc.
Boston, MA

WATERSKIING - Getting off the Ground! is designed to familiarize readers with matters of general interest relating to waterskiing. This book is presented for informational purposes and is not intended to constitute professional waterskiing instruction. ALL READERS SHOULD CONSULT WITH AND BE SUPERVISED BY A TRAINED PROFESSIONAL PRIOR TO ENGAGING IN ANY WATERSKIING ACTIVITY. The authors, publishers, and distributors assume no liability whatsoever in connection with the use of the information contained in this book.

Written by Mark B. Solomon
Edited by Gary B. Solomon

B&W photography by Robert Tannenbaum and Amy Lynn
Front cover top photograph by Mark Goldberg
Front cover bottom photograph by Amy Lynn
Back cover skiing photograph by Robert Tannenbaum

Graphic artwork by Mark B. Solomon
Shot on location at Camp Avoda, Middleboro, MA

Waterskiing equipment graciously provided by
Connelly Waterski

Special thanks to Paul G. Davis, Jason Kaplan, Tom Leavitt, Andrea Parker, Gregory Smith, and the Camp Avoda small craft department

Published by Aquatics Unlimited, Inc., Boston, MA.

Distributed by: ICS Books, Inc, 1370 E. 86th Place, Merrillville, IN 46410 (800) 541-7323

Printed in U.S.A.

Preface

The four sections of *WATERSKIING - Getting off the Ground!* are individual learning units. Each unit provides a complete skill set: waterskiing knowledge tools, waterskiing practical information, and waterskiing skills, and each unit builds upon the skills taught in the previous unit. The review questions and answers allow the student to measure his or her learning progress.

Beginner Section:
The Beginner Section is designed to educate the student in waterskiing fundamentals. At the end of the Beginner Section, the student should be able to assist the driver by performing all the functions of a spotter and get up on two skis! The student will also be introduced to tubing.

Advanced Section:
The Advanced Section is designed to educate the student in more active waterskiing issues. At the end of the Advanced section, the student should be able to exit and re-enter the wake, perform crest-to-crest wake crosses, and perform a dock start! The student will also be introduced to kneeboarding.

Driver Section:
The Driver Section is designed to educate the student in practical motorboat skills. At the end of the Driver section, the student, under supervision and with the aid of a crew, should be able to handle fuel and drive the motorboat (students with a valid automobile driver's license only) throughout a normal waterskiing day.

Slalom Section:
The Slalom Section is designed to educate the student in Slalom waterskiing techniques. At the end of the Slalom Section, the student should be able to stand on one ski, perform a deep water slalom start, perform crest-to-crest wake crosses, and throw a spray!

We dedicate this book to our parents, Barbara and Leonard Solomon, for providing us the opportunity to spend our childhood years at summer camp, for being our education role models, and for being so supportive throughout the entire *"WATERSKIING - Getting off the Ground!"* project.

Table of Contents

Table of Contents

Aquatics Unlimited presents _WATERSKIING - Getting off the Ground!_ and your waterskiing instructors, Gary and Mark.

Welcome aboard! Today we'll be learning the finer points of waterskiing: everything from motorboat nomenclature and fuel handling to the skier salute and throwing a spray.

Figure 1. Your waterskiing instructors, Mark and Gary

That's right, Mark. This will be an exciting day on the water, as always. We'll be covering all that you just mentioned and much more in our outdoor classroom. Don't worry if Mark's words sounded foreign; *by the end of this course, we'll all be speaking the same language.*

Figure 2. Slalom skiing

Beginner Introduction

- safety
- use of PFD
- clothing
- recommended safety equipment

Safety is just another word for common sense, and in waterskiing, as in all watersports, one must always be prepared for the unexpected.

Figure 3. Be prepared for the unexpected

I'm helping Lara put on a Type II **PFD**, or **personal flotation device**. We listen for the click, adjust the fit, and tie the top in a bow.

Figure 4. Listen for the click and adjust the fit

Figure 5. Secure the PFD by tying the top in a bow

Always be sure that you are wearing a PFD correctly rated for your weight. The PFD's weight rating can be found on the **Coast Guard label** located on the rear of the PFD.

The difference between Lara's **Type II PFD** and Gary's **Type III PFD** is head support. The Type II PFD is designed to keep the wearer's breathing passages clear of the water if the wearer should become unconscious. Young children, particularly those who have limited swimming ability, should wear a Type II PFD.

Figure 6. Unconscious boater with Type II PFD

11

While waterskiing, the skier should wear a Type III PFD rated for high impact protection because it provides more freedom of movement than the Type II PFD. The Type II PFD *should not be worn while waterskiing* because the head pad may actually slide over the skier's head and its straps could hurt the skier in the event of a

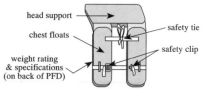

Figure 7. Type II PFD

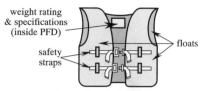

Figure 8. Type III PFD

hard fall. While riding on the boat, boat riders should decide whether to wear a Type II or Type III PFD based on their boating experience, swimming ability, and weather and water conditions. Maintain the PFD's safety qualities by hanging it to dry, keeping it clean, and especially not using it as a seat cushion. *Be good to your PFD; it may just save your life.*

Wearing **shoes** with nonskid soles protects feet from injury and reduces the likelihood of slipping on wet surfaces. In waterskiing, shoes help boat riders to board and deboard safely, to keep feet cool when walking on sun-exposed hot docks, and to guard feet from

injury due to shifting gear in the boat. When launching a boat from a trailer onto unfamiliar water, shoes or wetsuit neoprene booties will protect a boater's feet from potentially harmful debris on the shoreline, such as fish hooks and rocks.

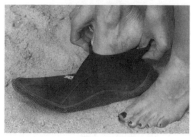

Figure 9. Neoprene booties

Figure 10. Nonskid sole shoes

A high-numbered, water-resistant **sunscreen** correct for the wearer's skin type should be applied before boating or waterskiing and should

be re-applied after waterskiing. **Sunglasses** with UV protection are a must to protect the eyes from water glare; sunglasses are especially important for drivers. A boat rider will find a sunglass strap to be convenient and to help prevent loss or damage.

Figure 11. Wear sunscreen

Figure 12. Wear sunglasses

Wearing appropriate **clothing** will make our boating experience more comfortable, but good judgement in this regard also protects us from such **medical conditions** as sunstroke, heat exhaustion, and hypothermia. For example, a wetsuit is mandatory skier gear when the air and water temperatures do not add up to 100°F (38°C). Even on warm water days, cool air or windy weather can make the skier uncomfortable, cause muscle cramps, or even cause hypothermia, which makes wearing a wetsuit a good idea. Dry towels and shirts should be kept on the boat to enable skiers to dry off and stay warm when riding on the boat after skiing.

Figure 13. Waterski clothing

13

Boat riders are encouraged to have warm and cold weather clothing available. Wearing a hat on sunny days will protect boat riders from a sunburn on the face and scalp. We recommend seeking current medical literature on the dangers that can result from prolonged exposure to the elements.

Figure 14. Appropriate waterskiing clothing and drinks

The required and recommended **safety equipment** is as important as proper protection from the elements. A prepared **Boat Captain**, the person responsible for the boat and safety of others on the boat, will always have a fire extinguisher and audible and visible distress signals available on the craft. Other items are also important for safety: bailer, spare PFD, extra line, heaving line, spare paddle, backboard, and anchor. Boaters traveling on large or unfamiliar waterways may be pleased to have equipped the boat with a map, two-way radio, depth finder, flare gun, flashlight, spare fuel line, extra fuel, various mechanical tools,

Figure 15. Audible and visible distress signals

food, and drinking water. Of course, remember a first aid kit. Consult with the local waterway authorities in the area in which you will be boating and waterskiing to be sure you know all the current rules, regulations, and water conditions. Note that most states require motorized craft to be registered annually.

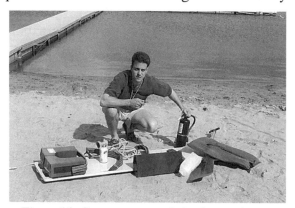

Figure 16. Some recommended safety equipment

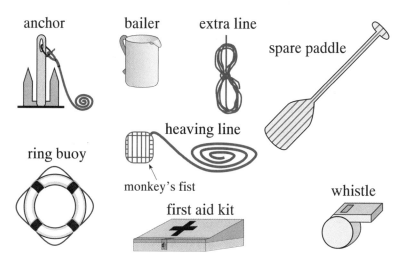

Figure 17. Recommended safety equipment

Common sense suggests knowing your limits. Recognize your abilities, and be aware of other craft, shallow water, rocks, and other obstructions. Always inform someone on shore that you are on the water and be sure to have proper supervision. Finally, be prepared to use the audible and visible distress signals in case of an emergency.

Beginner Tools

- boat nomenclature
- waterski nomenclature
- tow line nomenclature
- rolling hitch
- cleat hitch

Tools are important for getting a job done. **Motorboat nomenclature**, or names of parts of the boat, is a boater's most important communication tool. Let's review some motorboat nomenclature basics...

We'll begin with the general parts of the boat. The front of the motorboat is referred to as the bow. The rear of the boat is called the stern. The side to driver's left is the port - note that there are four letters in port and left - and the starboard is the side to the driver's right. The open area in which passengers sit is known as the cockpit, and the floor is referred to as the deck.

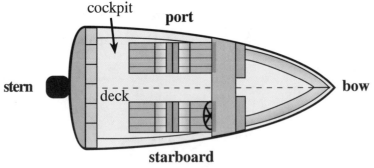

Figure 18. General boat nomenclature

Some specific parts of the boat are the seats, the steering wheel which is used to control the outboard engine's horizontal angle, the throttle which is used to control the direction (forward and reverse) and speed of the boat, the windshield which protects the driver, the gunnel or tops of the sides of the boat, the transom or the back wall of the boat, and, of course, the engine. Some boats are equipped with a tow line pole, to which the tow line is attached. A boom can be extended from the tow line pole over the side of a boat. Skiers can hold onto this boom, which will allow them to practice certain skills, such as getting up on two, one, or no skis.

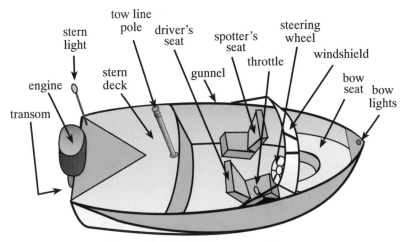

Figure 19. Specific boat nomenclature

Waterski nomenclature is also useful when communicating with other skiers. The front end of the ski is known as the tip, the boot is what holds the ski on the skier's foot, the boot adjustment mechanism allows the boots to be fitted to the skier's foot size, and the fin or skeg is the rounded blade located on the bottom of the ski. A ski with a boot and a slalom boot strap or two full boots is known as a slalom ski. An advanced waterskier places one foot in the front boot, and the other beneath the slalom boot strap (or in the second boot if the ski is so equipped) when skiing on only a slalom ski.

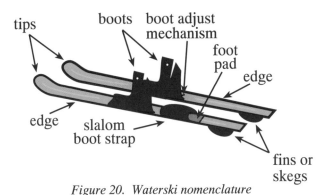

Figure 20. Waterski nomenclature

Other terms with which a Beginner Skier should be familiar is the **tow line nomenclature**. The tow line in its most basic form is composed of a long length of line that floats, and a handle with soft padding onto which the skier holds. Tow lines are typically made from polypropylene because this material floats. Often, the tow line connects to a traveler that rides along a tow line bridle. A traveler is a fancy pulley system, and a tow line bridle is a length of polypropylene line with strong clips on each end. These clips attach to eyebolts located on opposite ends of the transom. The bridle should be long enough to bring the traveler into the boat without disconnecting the clips.

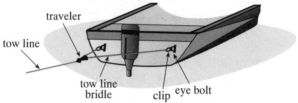

Figure 21. Tow line bridle and traveler assembly

Some boats are equipped with a tow line pole, mounted to a point on the centerline of the boat. By having the tow line pole extend higher than the engine, the line is unobstructed by the engine. This arrangement allows the tow line to simply swivel about the tow line pole when a skier is being towed.

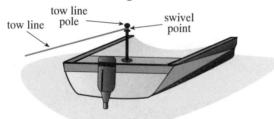

Figure 22. Tow line pole

Other words with which Beginner Skiers should become familiar are **motorboat movement terms**. If a motorboat is stationary in the water while the engine is running, it is often said to be in neutral. The propeller does not spin while in neutral, and consequently, the boat will not move in the water. If a motorboat is traveling backward (stern first), it is said to be in reverse. If a motorboat is traveling forward (bow first), it is said to be in forward. The period in which the motorboat goes from a stationary position to high speed is referred to as "accelerating out-of-the-hole", or accelerating out of neutral. **Accelerating** means to increase speed, and **decelerating** means to decrease speed. A boat turning to the left is said to be turning to port, and, of course, a boat turning to the right is said to be turning to starboard.

Boaters and waterskiers often find it useful to be able to tie knots and hitches during a day on the water. As good Beginner Skiers, we should become proficient in tying some simple knots. First, a piece of line has two ends: a standing end, which remains fixed,

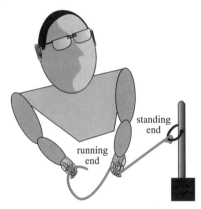

and a running end, which will be moving in our hands. Knots can be tied with the running end handled mainly by either the right or left hand; these are known as right-handed or left-handed knots, respectively. The knots demonstrated below are right-handed knots.

Figure 23. Line nomenclature

When a line is tied to a stationary object, the configuration tied to the object is known as a **hitch**, whereas a **knot** is a configuration in which the line is tied to itself. Two hitches often used to hold the boat to a dock are the rolling hitch and the cleat hitch.

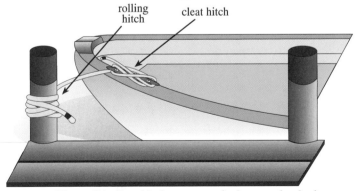

Figure 24. Two hitches secure the boat to the dock

The **rolling hitch** is useful for securing a boat to a dock pole because the rolling hitch will not slip. The rolling hitch is performed by making two turns around the pole with the running end - overlapping the standing end on each turn - and completed by making an underhand loop around the pole above the standing end.

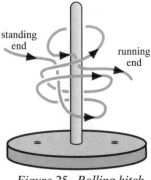

Figure 25. Rolling hitch illustration

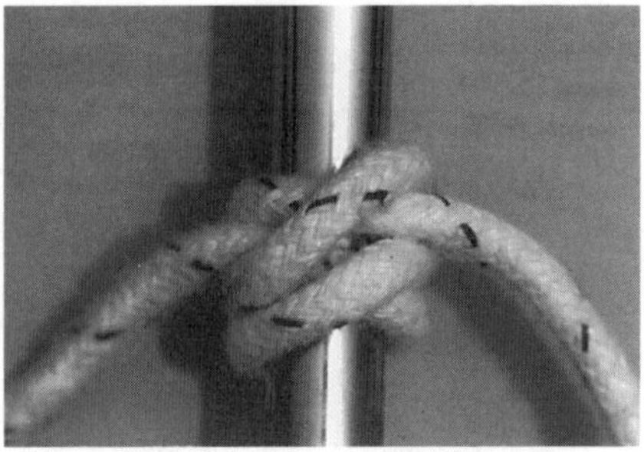

Figure 26. Rolling hitch photograph

To ensure the rolling hitch stays for a long period of time, the rolling hitch can be secured with two half-hitches. The two **half-hitches** are tied around the standing end with the excess length of running end. The first half-hitch is tied closer to the rolling hitch than the second half-hitch. The rolling hitch with two half-hitches is completed by tightening the half-hitches and sliding them against the rolling hitch.

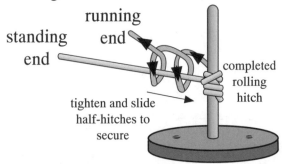

Figure 27. Rolling hitch with two half-hitches

A boater can attach the running end of the dock line to a cleat mounted on the boat. To tie a **cleat hitch**, begin with a circle, next make an "X", complete with an underhand turn such that the running end runs parallel to the line beneath it.

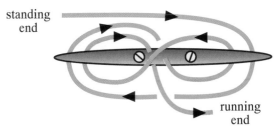

standing
end

running
end

Figure 28. Cleat hitch illustration

Figure 29. Cleat hitch photograph

The cleat hitch is used when **securing a boat to a dock**. Because the cleat hitch is the primary method of attaching a dock line to a boat, Beginners are encouraged to practice the cleat hitch until it can be performed with ease. When tying the boat to the dock, the length of line used should keep the side of the boat parallel to the dock. Boat bumpers, such as tires, can be used to protect the boat from being damaged or scratched by the dock. If the boat's side is not parallel to the dock after tying the bow and stern, the line lengths should be readjusted so that re-entering the boat will be easier and so that the boat can freely float, especially if boating in tidal waters.

Figure 30. Adjust line lengths

21

Beginner Practical

- swimming skills
- floating using a vest
- stretching
- boarding/deboarding

- skier signals (calls/hands/arms)
- entering the water (giant stride)
- re-entering the boat

Now that we have learned basic boating safety, language used to communicate with other boaters, and methods for securing a floating boat to a dock, we will prepare for our waterskiing exercises by learning associated skills fundamental to the sport and communication signals often used while waterskiing.

A minimum number of **swimming skills** are important to waterskiers for three reasons: first, a certain amount of swimming is required by a waterskier (such as when getting the tow line or retrieving a ski) even though skiers always wear a vest on the boat and in the water; second, swimming ability shows a certain level of fitness required to waterski; third, and most important, a skier must feel at ease in the water, especially while waiting for the craft to return after an unintentional fall.

It is recommended that the person responsible for the well-being of the waterskiers should test for the following specific swimming skills: two consecutive minutes of treading water, fifty yards (45

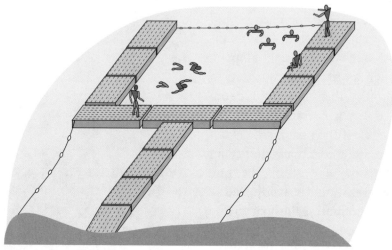

Figure 31. Treading water and swimming drills

meters) of the crawl stroke, and fifty yards (45 meters) of the breast stroke or freestyle. Once the waterskier candidate has successfully demonstrated those skills with reasonable competence, he or she should be given a Type III PFD to show his or her ability to float using a PFD. The waterskier should remain relaxed while floating. These drills or tests should be conducted *before* a person begins waterskiing lessons.

As in any sport, an athlete should take time to **warm-up** and **stretch** before engaging in the activity. Loosening arm, chest, neck, back, and especially leg and foot muscles will aid in preventing muscle cramps and pulls while skiing, and reduce muscle soreness after skiing. Waterskiing can be deceptive when it comes to the amount of physical exertion one uses while standing on the water.

Figure 32. Stretching calves and hamstrings

Figure 33. Stretching arms, shoulders, and back

Boarding and **deboarding** (moving between the dock and boat, respectively) a motorboat should be regarded as a skill. Before beginning, the engine must be off so that it does not accidently shift into gear while someone is boarding or deboarding. When boarding and deboarding any craft, we "shift our weight" as we step behind our hands. Notice that Gary holds onto both the point of entry and exit, which holds the boat close to the dock and also keeps his weight low. Keeping one's weight low improves balance on a boat, and a boat's balance on the water. After the first person has boarded the craft, the other crew members, who aided in holding the boat against the dock, pass gear into the craft to be stowed by the person aboard.

Figure 34. Boarding, stay low and shift weight into boat

Before going waterskiing, all persons should be familiar with the **skier communication signals**, which include audible, hand, and arm signals that the skier will use to indicate his or her status and requests to those in the boat. There are three situations in which skier communication signals are used: (1) when the waterskier is preparing to get pulled up, (2) while the waterskier is skiing, and (3) after the waterskier has released or fallen. The two people who will use these signals are the skier and **spotter**, who is the designated person on the boat watching the skier at all times and communicating with the skier on occasion. It is important that the driver keeps his hands on the wheel at all times and has his attention forward, so no communication between the skier and driver is possible.

When the skier is preparing to get pulled up out of the water, **audible skier signals** can be used because the engine is relatively quiet in neutral and there is no wind noise created by the boat's movement. Before accelerating out of neutral after the skier has the tow line handle, the spotter will call to the skier, "Ready?!". The skier will respond with an audible signal of either "WAIT!" or "HIT IT!" The word "GO!" is never used because it sounds too similar to "NO!" If the skier has only the tow line rather than the handle in his or her hands when the boat accelerates out-of-the-hole, the skier's hands will be sure to get a serious rope burn or abrasion. A worse situation could develop if the skier is actually entangled in the tow line when the craft accelerates. So, the boat will only accelerate out-of-the-hole to towing speed upon the command signal "HIT IT!" initiated by the skier.

Figure 35. Skier indicates to the boat when ready

We will now discuss the set of **hand signals** used while the skier is waterskiing. Because of engine noise, the only practical means of communication between the boat and skier is through hand signals. Three of the four hand signals from the skier to the spotter are for boat speed adjustment. These signals are "thumbs up" meaning 'speed up the boat', "thumbs down" meaning 'slow down the boat', or "okay", which means 'this is a good speed for me.'

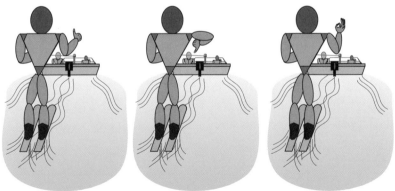

Figure 36. Faster   *Figure 37. Slower*   *Figure 38. Speed is Okay*

The last hand signal a skier sometimes transmits to the boat is a "slash across the neck," indicating 'release', which means the skier is about to release from the tow line by simply releasing his or her grip from the handle.

Figure 39. Release

The spotter, too, has a set of hand and arm signals to communicate with the skier while the skier is underway. The **spotter signals** include a "waves" signal, where the horizontally positioned hand goes up and down to indicate the boat (and then the skier) is about to cross through waves large enough to disturb the boat.

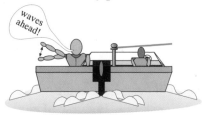

Figure 40. Spotter signals waves

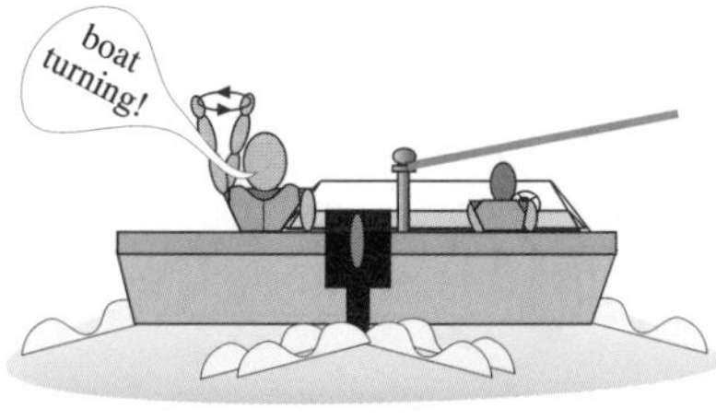

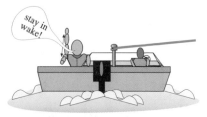

Figure 41. Spotter signals turning

The spotter's vertically positioned hand and arm that rotates clockwise or counterclockwise indicates the boat is going to turn to the right or left, respectively.

Finally, a spotter's hand and arm that repeatedly points directly behind the boat then to the sky indicates that the skier should get directly behind the boat until further notice.

Figure 42. Skier to stay in wake

Other hand and arm signals can be developed by the group for use while a skier is behind the boat for safety, skiing style, or anything else. The basic idea is that everyone, on the boat and skiing, must be aware of the meaning of all signals.

The third set of skier communication signals are **arm signals**, used by a skier after he or she has released the tow line or accidentally fallen. Two arms in the air making an "O" indicates "I'm Okay." A spotter receiving an "I'm Okay" signal should give the driver this information because the driver bases his driving on the skier's condition. "I'm Okay" is usually an indication that the skier wishes to continue.

Figure 43. Universal signal - I am "okay"

Only one waving arm means, "I need pickup." An "I need pickup" is a level of higher immediacy for the driver, where returning to the skier is just a little quicker. "I need pickup" could mean the skier is slightly injured or merely tired and ready to re-enter the boat. Skiers and spotters wishing to distinguish between two physical conditions could create another arm signal.

Figure 44. Universal signal - I need assistance

No skier communication signal combined with little skier movement (and often the skier's head raised back or drooped forward) means the skier has suffered an injury, so pickup is urgent. The driver should return to the skier as quickly as is safely possible, and those in the craft should be prepared to assist the skier. The post ski communication signals should be performed every time the skier has ended his or her run to keep everyone on the craft informed of his or her physical condition.

Figure 45. Universal signal - return as quickly as possible

Now that we have completed learning the skier communication signals and practiced those drills, let's move to a more interesting and dynamic skill: entering the water from the boat.

Entering the water can be easy, fun, and safe when the proper technique is used. First, the engine is turned off to ensure the propeller is not spinning while someone is in the water nearby the boat. Next, the Type III PFD should be checked to be sure it fits snugly. When entering the water, the skier *always* jumps feet-first because the depth of the water and possible existence of underwater debris are not always known; diving into shallow water can cause serious head and neck injury.

Experienced skiers often choose to use the giant stride when entering the water, rather than simply jumping into the water. To perform a **giant stride**, the skier jumps into the water with one leg angled forward and one leg angled back. Upon the feet striking the water, the legs are snapped together, squeezing the water inward, which creates an upward force on the skier. During the jump, the skier's arms start crossed in front of the chest, then sweep outward along the water's surface once the arms make contact with the water. Proficient skiers are able to perform the giant stride well enough to keep their heads above the water's surface altogether. Finally, a skier can use alternate forms of water entry if the boat has a ladder or transom platform, but, again, feet-first entry should always be observed.

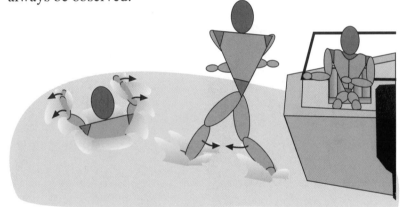

Figure 46. Entering the water with a giant stride

Before skiing is started, all persons responsible for the skiers should be sure that the skier is comfortable with the floating-in-a-vest skill. Young children or weak swimmers (who have passed the swimming requirement tests) will have an easier time learning to be comfortable floating in a vest in shallow water, rather than out in the deep water.

At the end of a **run** (i.e., a reasonably long period of waterskiing), the skier must re-enter the motorboat. One method for **re-entering the craft** is to reach up to the port or starboard gunnel, perform the flutter kick used in the crawl stroke, or whip kick used in the breast stroke (whichever is found to be more effective), and pull up until balancing on the hands over the gunnel with legs resting against the outside of the boat. From this position, the skier can quickly maneuver into a position where he or she is sitting on the gunnel to enable a simple swivel turn to step onto the deck. Very agile skiers can kick one foot onto the gunnel from the hand balancing position and hop into the boat. Others may need assistance to get to the hand balancing position, so the spotter can pull upward on the ski vest shoulders. Small children can simply be lifted by the forearms into the craft - lift gently.

Figure 47. Getting into the boat - kick & pull technique

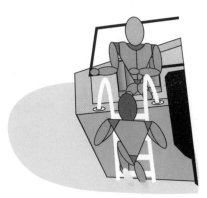

An easier method for re-entering the motorboat from the water is to climb a sturdy ladder, which can be installed on the transom. There are also boats that have a small platform extending from the transom at the water level that can make re-entry an easy task. Whichever method of re-entry is to be performed, the driver must *always turn the engine off* to ensure the skier's safety.

Figure 48. Getting into the boat - ladder climb technique

Beginner Skiing Skills

- putting on skis
- floating with skis
- swimming with skis
- getting the tow line
- tandem deep water start
- tandem standing position
- parts of the wake
- tandem moving left & right
- tandem run release
- falling
- tubing

We've learned safety considerations in the Beginner Introduction section, nomenclature in the Beginner Tools section, and communication techniques in the Beginner Practical section. In the Beginner Skiing Skills section, we will be using all that we have learned and add skills necessary for making the time in the water easier, as well as learning an effective method for getting pulled up onto waterskis. The key to success for all new and inexperienced skiers is patience; movement in the water when handling and wearing skis must be performed more slowly than on land so as not to use excess energy in getting the skis on and getting ourselves into skiing position.

After the skier has set the waterski boots correctly for his or her foot size, while on the boat, and entered the water (possibly using a giant stride), the skis can be passed into the water for the skier, who is now floating in a vest. When **passing the skis to a skier** a short distance away from the boat, each ski can be glided on its bottom, tip first, with a gentle push by the spotter or other passenger. For a skier next to the boat, the ski can simply be laid on the water within the skier's reach.

Figure 49. Sliding skis to the skier

If the skier has both skis in the water with him or her, the ski not being put on by the skier should be set **boot-side down** so that wind does not move it away from the skier. Note that the boot in the water prevents the ski from drifting away from the skier.

Figure 50. Place one ski 'boot side down'

Once the skier is resting comfortably in the water and allowing the ski vest to do its flotation work, the skier is ready for the 'putting on the skis' exercise. A waterski can be worn on either foot without regard to left or right. While **putting on a ski**, the skier lays back and brings his or her knees to the water's surface. The first ski is then held perpendicular to the water's surface with the boot approximately at the water's surface. The skier will spread the ski boot to allow his or her foot to slide into the boot. Most boots are designed with finger holes that allow the skier to spread the boot easily. The skier stays in that reclined position with knees bent and ski tip to the sky. The second ski is then held vertical with

Figure 51. Lean back to put on waterski

boot spread until it is on the skier's other foot. The order in which the skis are put on - either left or right foot first - is totally up to the skier. Above all else, the skier must be comfortable during all phases of the 'putting on the ski' exercise. We should note that most modern ski boots have an adjustment mechanism, meaning the boot will stay in position when slid to fit a smaller foot size. This **boot adjustment mechanism** allows a skier to adjust the boot for a large foot size, slide his or her foot easily into the boot, and slide the boot to fit his or her foot. Making these adjustments in the water takes a little practice but can save wear and tear on the boot and may be easier for some skiers. The goal - no matter which method is used to adjust the boot to the skier's foot - either pre-fitting on the boat or in-the-water fitting - is to have the boot fit snugly on the skier's foot so that the skier feels confident that the boot will stay on while skiing.

Figure 52. Adjust boot size mechanism to fit foot

Floating with skis on one's feet can be easy or difficult. The easy and relaxing method is to lie back with knees at the water's surface and ski tips high out of the water, pointing to the sky. The difficult and tiring method for a skier is to allow the skis to turn sideways or to float on his or her stomach. Should we find ourselves in such an awkward position, we can bring our knees toward our chest and roll onto our back. Once in the relaxing floating position, we can use gentle arm motions on the water's surface to maintain balance.

Often, **swimming with skis** is required to reach the tow line. An efficient method for swimming with skis is to maintain the floating position while swimming backward, and sweeping our arms from our side toward our knees. Keeping hands cupped to push the maximum amount of water will add power to this modified back stroke.

Figure 53. Hand paddle backward to tow line

The reason floating with skis is an important skill with which to be comfortable is because that position will be held most of the time a skier spends in the water. The tow line can be brought to the skier only after the skis are securely on the skier's feet, and, because of the nature of tow lines, it may take the driver a little time to properly move the tow line into position for the skier. Also, because of wind and other variations, the skier often may find the swimming-backward skill quite useful. Therefore, after putting waterskis on in water for the first time, the skier should take a few minutes to get familiar with the 'relaxing on the back' and 'swimming backward' exercises.

The tow line handle rarely arrives at the skier before the tow line, half-way between the boat and the handle, arrives. Herein lies the next skill which a Beginner Skier must learn - **sliding the tow line between the hands**. When the driver is taking the tow line past the skier and into starting position, the driver must take heed to move the line slowly enough to enable the skier to handle it. The skier's role is to

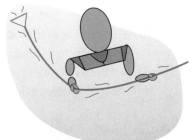

Figure 54. Sliding tow line between hands

allow the line to slide across his or her cupped hands while waiting for the handle to which he or she may grip. Attempting to hold the tow line by any part other than the handle can cause rope burn, abrasion, or even a cut. A skier who grips the tow line rather than allowing it to slide through his or her hands will also be turned from the desired position, which is feet-first, facing the boat.

Once the skier hears or feels the tow line handle approaching, he may wish to call out, "neutral!" to indicate that the driver should put the engine into neutral to allow the skier to take hold of the handle without being pulled forward dramatically. After the skier has a firm grip on the handle and is facing the boat in a relaxed position, the skier may call, "take up the slack!", which indicates that the driver should reengage into the slowest forward speed until the tow line is taut between the boat and the skier. At this point, the skier is in a relaxed sitting position with the tow line passing between his or her skis, knees bent and out of the water, tips vertical and high out of the water with skis parallel.

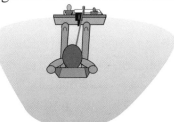

Figure 55. Tow line is placed between skis

Once the tow line is taut, the spotter calls to the skier, "Ready?", and the skier, if ready for the driver to start the boat forward, calls "Hit it!" Otherwise, a "wait!" call is made by the skier and the spotter instructs the driver accordingly. The driver will be able to

Figure 56. Tandem-ski deep water start

hear the skier's commands, too, but since the driver's attention is always forward, he or she should get the final word from his rear-looking eyes, the spotter.

When the skier does call "Hit it!", the skier holds the handle tightly, maintains the sitting position, and casually allows the boat to pull him or her to a standing position on the water - and away we go, "Getting off the Ground!"

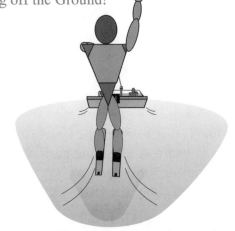

Figure 57. Wait for enough speed to stand

When performing a **tandem deep water start**, the Beginner Skier should not feel pressured to hold onto the handle. If an extreme amount of force is required to hold onto the handle, the skier should release it. The extreme amount of force may be due to the skier's losing his or her balance or unintentionally letting the ski tips go below the water's surface, which may even cause the skier to burrow through the water. Sometimes Beginner Skiers have a difficult time distinguishing 'normal drag while getting-up' from 'burrowing', but will undoubtedly learn through experience.

The skier who has successfully achieved the standing position will have noticed that at a certain point, the skis rotated from a vertical position to a horizontal position relative to the water's surface. When the skis are horizontal on the water's surface, the skis are said to be 'planing' on the water. To stand on planing skis requires very little energy compared to that used in the period between sitting in the water and planing.

There is no exact science to a tandem deep water start. The best recommendation is to stay balanced and be patient; trying to stand too fast results in being pulled forward, slipping backward, or rocking sideways. While the boat is building speed, we should concentrate on keeping the skis parallel - about shoulder length apart with tips directly in front of us to enable the skis beneath us to plane on the water's surface. The trick is to allow the boat and skis to do the work.

Let's watch Gary perform a deep water tandem ski start. We should observe his body position during start-up. Gary begins in sitting position with knees bent, keeping the skis parallel and pointing to the sky with the tips well out of the water. As the boat picks up speed, Gary concentrates on maintaining his feet about shoulder-width apart, holding the grip tightly while bending the

Figure 58. Skis parallel, tips up, knees bent, feet shoulder width

arms slightly at the elbow, and keeping his back straight. Experienced skiers will make corrections to balance by pulling the arms into the chest or extending their arms while maintaining their body position.

Figure 59. Knees bent, back straight, adjust with arms

Gary is demonstrating the effect of trying to stand too quickly and illustrating how to pull arms into the chest to correct balance to result in a successful start. Normally, however, skiers will maintain their initial arm position with only minor adjustments until the skis are planing.

Figure 60. Be patient until planing

Once **standing on two skis**, experienced waterskiers relax, keep their knees slightly bent to act as shock absorbers, concentrate on keeping the back straight, and keep feet shoulder-width apart. These body positions are meant to better the skier's balance on the skis and to minimize stress on the back.

Figure 61. Standing on planing waterskis

We should remember that if the boat's speed is not to our liking, we can let the spotter know by giving the thumbs up or thumbs down to increase or decrease the boat's speed, respectively. When the speed is right for us, we give the "Okay" signal to let both spotter and driver know to hold the boat's speed constant.

Immediately after starting up, the skier will find him or herself **skiing inside the wake**. The wake is the area behind the moving motorboat that is between the first big waves created by the boat's hull displacing the water over which the boat passes. The wake starts as wide as the hull immediately behind the motorboat, and spreads as the boat moves farther from that point on the water.

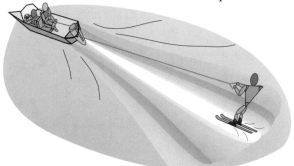

Figure 62. Once standing, keep knees bent, shoulders back, back straight, elbows slightly bent

Beginner Skiers should also be familiar with **wake nomenclature**. The center of the wake is often called the turbulence zone. This turbulence zone appears to be the strip of water that made contact with the motor and propeller because of the many air bubbles and large currents found there. The large peaks that define the wake are the port and starboard wake crests. Immediately outside the port and starboard wake crests are the port and starboard wake troughs, respectively. Between the turbulence zone and port or starboard crests is a smooth area, which is often a region protected from large waves or other boats' wakes. All boats produce different wake shapes and sizes. The sizes of the crests and troughs, for instance, vary inversely with the hull displacement, where a boat that rides deeper in the water than another boat is said to have greater hull displacement; its wake crests will, in turn, be larger than the boat having less hull displacement.

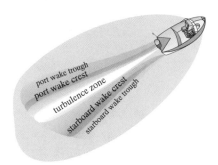

Figure 63. Wake nomenclature

Now that we know how to stand on skis, we should begin **controlling left and right movement**. A good drill is to move back and forth to the smooth areas inside the wake. To move left, the skier gently takes pressure off his or her left foot. To move right, the skier gently takes pressure off his or her right foot. Advance with this skill at a comfortable pace; with practice and patience, moving left and right will become very natural.

Figure 64. Move side-to-side in wake

At the end of the run, assuming the run did not end due to a fall, the waterskier will give the spotter a "release" hand signal (hand across the neck) then simply release his or her grip on the handle. Spotters should respond with an "Okay" hand signal unless there is a better or more suitable place for the waterskier to release immediately ahead. After the release, the skier can practice his or her balancing act, then slowly sink into the refreshing water.

Figure 65. Release tow line and cool down

Though a **fall** is never comfortable, an experienced skier will try to minimize the effects of a fall by attempting to keep his or her head out of the water while at the same time getting his or her back onto the water's surface. A well padded ski vest helps to protect the body from impact with the water. Skiers who impact their ski may want to board the boat to check for any cuts that may have been caused by the impact. A person whose head enters the water first, while the rest of the body is above water, will usually find him or herself feeling the effects of the fall manifested as a stiff neck.

For those who are not completely comfortable as waterski persons or for those waterski persons who would like a relatively relaxing ride, air-filled circular tubes are a great way to go. This is known as **tubing**.

Figure 66. Tubing can be fun and relaxing!

Most tubes that are designed to be pulled behind a motorboat are well constructed, durable material encasing an innertube, and provide a bottom in the center of the tube. There is also a place of extra durable construction to which the tow line attaches. In addition, special grabloops are located in the front, which are both functional and comfortable to hold, as we shall see. Inflating a tube is most easily performed by using an electric pump (never used near water) and inflated until the tube is firm; over-inflation can damage the innertube, but under-inflation will not support a tube rider on the water very well. Sinking into the water during start-up is an indication that the tube needs additional air.

The first skill **tube riders,** or tubers, must master is **tube mounting**. This may be performed from the boat (by holding the tube firmly against the boat for stability), or from the water (by reaching up from the water at the back of the tube and performing several kicks to advance toward the front where the tow line attaches). As good Beginners, we know that wearing a Type III PFD when tubing is just as important as when waterskiing.

Figure 67. Climbing on the tube from the boat

Once the tube rider has successfully climbed onto the tube, he or she can choose to ride on his or her stomach or back. In either case, the tube rider's head should be positioned so as to be able to look forward to watch the boat and look for waves.

As suggested, most tubes provide tube grabloops on the side the line attaches. The reason for grabloops being placed on the area in which the line attaches to the tube is so that, as the rider holds onto the

Figure 68. Hold tight and keep front up

grabloops, the leading edge of the tube raises upward, helping to force the water beneath the tube. This upward angle in the direction of travel helps provide stability.

In terms of safety, one should avoid wrapping hands or arms in any line or loop attached to the tube or tow line in order to prevent injury in the event a tube rollover occurs. If a rollover does occur, the tube rider should release his or her grip on the grabloops, while at the same time the spotter should alert the driver, who will slow and turn the boat to return for the tube rider. The driver, tuber, and

Figure 69. A turning boat causes the tube to slide sideways

spotter must be aware of the tuber's experience, and ability, which means to keep the boat at a slow enough speed (e.g., between 15 and 25mph) to enable the tuber to hang on, especially when crossing waves.

Figure 70. Fun on and off the water

Of course, no ride is ever complete without taking a few minutes to sit back and relax. The same principle of keeping the leading side of the tube raised applies while relaxing.

Figure 71. Sitting position - keep feet high

A driver will take the tube rider for a long meandering ride along a scenic portion of the waterway.

Figure 72. Sitting position - relax and enjoy the ride

After getting the hang of the tube, one can have a rather good time!

Once the tube rider has ridden the tube on his or her stomach and back, meandered around the shoreline, crossed the wake, and bounced over a few large waves, it will be time to again focus on improving waterskiing skills.

Beginner Review

1. **PFD Types**. Describe the differences between Type II and Type III PFDs.

2. **Recommended Safety Equipment**. (a) Make a list of five or more pieces of safety equipment that would be important for general safety or an emergency event. (b) Can you think of equipment not discussed?

3. **Boat Nomenclature**. (a) Name the four general areas of a boat. (b) Name specific parts of the motorboat.

4. **Waterski Nomenclature**. Name the parts of the waterski. (Hint: draw a waterski and label it).

5. **Pre-ski Audible Signals**. (a) What words will a skier use to indicate preparedness, or lack thereof, for the driver to accelerate the craft after the skier has received the handle in preparation for a deep water start? (b) Can you remember the two words we should not use in this situation?

6. **Skier Hand Signals and Spotter Arm Signals**. We discussed communication signals the skier and spotter could use to overcome the engine and wind noise. (a) What are the skiers four basic hand signals and what do they mean? (b) What are the spotters three basic arm signals and what do they mean?

7. **Fallen Skier Arm Signals**. (1) One arm waving in the air means, "I _____." (b). Two arms forming a circle in the air means, "I'm _____." (c) No raised arms means, "I _____."

8. **Skier's Stance**. (a) When performing a deep water start, the skier should pretend to be leaning way back in a rocking chair with knees very bent, arms slightly bent, and back straight. Describe the skis relative to each other, the water's surface, and the boat during a deep water start. (b) Describe the body position and waterskis relative to each other when skiing on tandem (two) skis.

9. **Parts of the Motorboat Wake**. We discussed the parts of the wake. Can you draw a moving motorboat with a wake and label the parts of the wake?

10. **Moving Left and Right Inside the Wake**. In the Beginner Skiing section, we learned how to control left and right movement inside the wake across the turbulence zone. To move left, we take pressure off our (left / right) ski. (circle the correct choice).

Bonus:
(a) Tie a rolling hitch.
(b) Tie a cleat hitch using only one hand.

We're now one step along toward Getting off the Ground!

Advanced Tools

- other ski equipment: wetsuit, drysuit, gloves
- knots: square knot, sheetbend, bowline

In the Beginner Section, we learned about wearing PFDs whenever waterskiing or in a boat. Since we will be spending more time waterskiing as Advanced Tandem Skiers, let's look at other equipment waterskiers have available.

When the air or water temperature is colder than comfortable, and always when the air and water temperatures do not add up to 100° Fahrenheit (38°C), experienced waterskiers wear a wetsuit. A **wetsuit**, usually (1/8" (6mm) thick or less for waterskiing) is made of neoprene, which is a stretchable material. The wetsuit is designed to fit snugly around the body in order to hold a film of water between the suit and skier's skin. This film of water will warm to body temperature which, in turn, keeps the skin and body warm. The

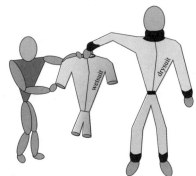

Figure 73. Wetsuit and drysuit

few seconds of chill while filling the wetsuit with chilly water is worth the warmth the wetsuit will provide. In contrast, a drysuit will not allow any water onto the skin beyond the tight cuffs at the wrists and ankles, however, a wetsuit is more appropriate for waterskiing.

Figure 74. Wetsuit apparel: shorts, shorty, and full length

Another piece of waterskiing apparel skiers may find useful are waterskiing gloves. **Waterskiing gloves** keep hands warm and provide more gripping power for the tow line handle than do bare hands. Gloves vary in style, material, and size. A good pair of comfortable gloves can enhance one's skiing performance.

Figure 75. Wetsuit, Type III PFD, gloves, and booties

In the Beginner Section, we learned the cleat hitch and rolling hitch to keep the boat held to the dock. Three knots often used by boaters for performing various tasks are the square knot, the sheet bend, and the bowline.

Right over left then left over right makes the **square knot**. The square knot is useful for tying gear to the craft. A square knot can always be untied by simply pushing one of the small loops forward, such that the line forming the large loop and the line used to make the other small loop are loosened.

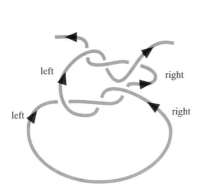

Figure 76. Square knot illustration

Figure 77. Square knot photograph

If we want to tie two pieces of line together, we should use the square knot's cousin, the **sheet bend**. The sheet bend is tied like the square knot, but rather than bringing the running end through the loop, the running end gets passed between the loop and the standing end.

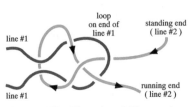

Figure 78. Sheet bend illustration

Figure 79. Sheet bend photograph

The **bowline** is used for making a temporary loop at the end of a line for uses such as a temporary dock line. To tie a bowline, we hold the standing end away from ourselves, then twist an overhand loop with the running end hand's thumb and forefinger. Then, with the running end, "the rabbit comes out of the hole, goes around the tree, and jumps back into the hole." The bowline is another knot that can always be untied by rotating the small loop forward.

Figure 80. Bowline illustration

Figure 81. Bowline photograph

48

Advanced Practical

- tossing the line
- coiling the line
- driver/spotter/skier responsibilities
- person overboard
- down skier rescue
- artificial respiration

As good Advanced Practical members of the boat crew, we should be familiar with handling the tow line, because that will be one of our main responsibilities. The most important idea to learn is how to keep the tow line untangled and knot free. The two tow line skills useful in the boat are the tow line toss and the tow line take-in.

Let's watch as Gary performs the **tow line toss.** We see he picks up the line just behind the handle with his throwing arm, and holds some line to go out with the toss in his other hand. He then steps to the side of the boat, twirls the handle a few times on the outside of the boat, and releases the handle, sending it and as much of the line as he can behind the boat. Gary takes care that he is standing away from the line on the boat deck so as not to get rope burn as it carries outward. Once the handle is in the water, the driver puts the boat into the lowest gear forward and the line is

Figure 82. Swing handle over water

Figure 83. Release tow line and let fly

49

guided out while making sure no knots develop in the line. The tow line bridle and traveler are then helped over the engine. Another method is to simply separate the handle away from the bulk of the line, toss it all overboard, and put the boat into forward to make the line extend. Care should be taken when using this method so that a knot is not placed in the line and tightened when pulling a skier.

The **tow line take-in** consists of a crew member pulling in the line using a hand-over-hand motion, allowing the line to fall on the deck between his or her feet, and separating the handle from the rest of the line.

Figure 84. Tow line toss overview

Coiling the line neatly on the boat tends to result in knots in the line more often than does random distribution of the line, though coiling the line neatly when hanging in dry storage is preferable to having a bulk of line left in a corner.

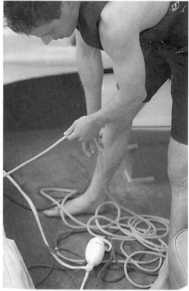

Figure 85. Haul in line without coiling

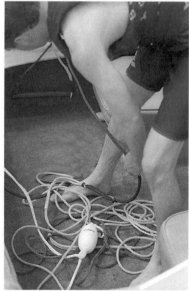

Figure 86. Separate handle from line

Safety is everyone's concern. The **driver/spotter/skier respon-sibilities** are important for the safety of the skier and the boat riders. Let's look at each person's role in helping to keep one another out of harm's way while enjoying a day on the water.

As driver, Mark keeps his attention forward, scanning the water for swimmers, boats, and other potential waterway hazards. The driver should remain seated while driving, so as not to accidentally lose control of the craft. The driver may also find it necessary to wear sunglasses to enable viewing through the sun's glare from the water.

Figure 87. Standard driver/spotter sitting positions

The spotter's main responsibilities are to communicate messages between the skier and driver (such as faster or slower from the skier and waves or turning direction from the driver) and to alert the driver of the skier's status (such as skier on port or starboard and, especially, skier down!). The spotter, too, should remain seated at all times while the motorboat is in motion.

The skier's responsibilities are twofold: to have fun while skiing and to watch for potential hazards to his or her person. Such hazards include rocks, weeds, tree branches, buoys, and other boats. Keep in mind that all people on the craft have done a pre-ski scouting for hazards on the waterway to minimize risk, so the skier can concentrate on skiing.

In the event a boat rider falls into the water unexpectedly, the now **person overboard** may be panicking, especially if that person was not safety-conscious and is not wearing a PFD. The most important idea to remember in such a case is to reach the victim by any means, without physically getting into the water. A panicking person will grab 'anything floating'; a rescuer on the water's surface represents 'anything floating' and may be grabbed by the panicking person and held underwater, even by a small child. The best method is for the driver to approach the person overboard on the driver's side - so as to

Figure 88. Rescuing an overboard victim

maintain visual contact - then for the spotter to reach to the victim - using a ring buoy with line attached, the tow line, a spare paddle, a spare PFD, or even a waterski. *Never enter the water without proper lifeguard training and then only enter with the proper rescue equipment.*

Unfortunate accidents can occur while waterskiing. Two such accidents are **neck and back injuries**. These problems must be taken seriously or permanent damage may occur to the victim. The method for handling the victim is to keep the victim's head from turning from the position in which the victim is found, and to move the victim slowly. For a victim floating in the water, first, rotate the victim onto his or her back by placing one arm along the spine and holding the head in place with that arm's hand. The other arm is placed along the chest and also supports the head while rotating the body. Next, a backboard is floated up to the victim's back and the victim is secured to the board, paying particular care not to rotate or arch the neck. A properly equipped waterfront should have a backboard that has head and neck immobilization pads and straps to secure a victim's head, chest, arms, and legs.

All boat captains should be trained and rehearsed in the use of these **backboards**. The best place to handle the victim is where a rescue team can stand, rather than in deep water. However, there may be no option so, as good Advanced Practical members, we should practice this maneuver in both shallow and deep water.

Figure 89. Rehearsing the proper use of a backboard

In a real **emergency situation**, we would seek immediate medical care, and, above all else, limit the victim's movement. Once ashore, place the victim in a cool area and pay attention to signs of any breathing difficulty. Note that this guide to handling a down skier with neck or back injury is simply a guide, and it is mandatory to have proper medical training through the Red Cross, medical literature, or from a medical practitioner.

Artificial respiration knowledge is important in waterskiing because of the potential danger found in the sport. As always, be prepared by knowing Red Cross standards, learning current medical artificial respiration techniques, and using common sense.

Figure 90. Artificial respiration discussion

Advanced Skiing Skills

- leaving the wake
- entering the wake
- crossing the wake
- waterskiing drills

- dock start
- skier salute
- knee boarding

In the Beginner Skiing Section, we learned how to control left and right movement when standing behind the boat inside its wake by reducing pressure on the left and right ski, respectively. In the Advanced Skiing Skills Section, we will learn and practice crossing the wake, begin balancing on one ski (in preparation for slalom skiing), and be introduced to kneeboarding. Skiers who are not yet comfortable with controlling their position behind the craft so as to remain in the wake during a turn, should practice that exercise before continuing.

There are three methods for **crossing a wake crest**. The first method is to slide across the wake crest so that one ski at a time passes over the crest. The second method is to be more assertive and angle the skis more toward the direction of movement. The third is the most aggressive where the skis are angled virtually perpendicular to the wake and a high speed is held all the way through the first crest and across the second crest. These three ways to cross a wake reflect the learning progression experienced by typical tandem skiers.

When crossing the wake crest, be affirmative; simply keep the pressure off the turn-to ski the entire way with knees bent to absorb

Figure 91. Crossing the wake

the bump while crossing over the wake. The same is true when re-entering the wake. The best method for becoming comfortable with crossing in and out of the wake is to do it repeatedly along a straight run. New Advanced Skiers should coordinate this drill with the driver and spotter before beginning a run. Also, drivers should still take wide, gentle turns for new Advanced Skiers at this point, as we are concentrating on exiting and re-entering the wake.

As Mark demonstrates **leaving the wake** while on two skis, he reduces pressure on his turn-to ski, to initiate the directional change, and continues through the crest of the wake. Skiers who need to work on their tandem skiing balance may want to avoid the situation of having one ski in the wake and one ski outside the wake because the skis will tend to separate and affect his or her balance. Later, when skiers become more comfortable with crossing the wake and balance improves, they invariably enjoy playing on and around the wake crest.

Figure 92. Beside the wake

To begin **re-entering the wake**, reducing pressure on the wake-side ski will steer the skier back into the wake. Bent knees and affirmative thinking will take the skier cleanly back into the wake; balance, confidence, and practice will soon make moving out of and back into the wake very natural.

Figure 93. Turning to re-enter wake

Figure 94. Relax while crossing into the wake

After becoming comfortable with getting out of and back into the wake and skiing outside the wake, the skier should turn the ski tips more toward the wake crests when exiting and re-entering, such that the wake-side ski edges dig into the water. The skier should try to hold that position into and all the way across the wake. To angle the skis toward the wake, simply take more pressure off the inside ski and lean into the turn. While crossing the wake, the skier should look across the wake, not at his or her skis.

Figure 95. Slowly move across the wake

Figure 96. Bend knees and arms for waves and line slack

Watch as Gary demonstrates **crossing the wake** at a more pronounced angle. He reduces inside ski pressure, turns into the wake, keeps his shoulders squared to his skiing direction, and looks across the wake. Once on the other side, Gary will reduce pressure on his new inside ski and lean back toward the wake to cross back to the other side. Remember, balance and progressing at your own pace are the winning ingredients in waterskiing.

Figure 97. Continue across wake

Figure 98. Exit other side of wake

An Advanced Skier can become more comfortable with his or her skills of crossing the wake by skiing from just beyond the trough of the port wake crest to just beyond the trough of the starboard wake crest, in repetition. This practicing will enhance the Advanced Skier's confidence and ability to turn. Placing pressure on the outside ski will aid in stopping the skier's motion away from the wake and start the turn back into the wake. As

Figure 99. Keep arms comfortable

the skier becomes more comfortable with making the wake cross, he or she should shift weight toward the wake (without adding pressure to the inside ski) and bend at the knees. Maintaining a straight back by keeping the shoulders back and waist straight will help to reduce pressure on the back and stomach, while allowing the knees to act as shock absorbers.

Figure 100. Practice exiting both sides of wake

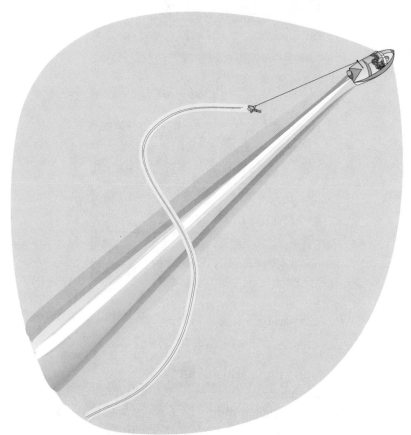

Figure 101. Continuous wake crossing improves confidence and turning skill

Often times, the water outside the wake will not be as smooth as the water inside the wake due to wind or the wakes of other boats. The skier will find that keeping knees bent, feet shoulder-wide, and staying relaxed will smoothen the ride when **skiing over waves**. When encountering particularly large waves, a method for traversing them (if unable to hide inside the wake) is to bend the knees, broaden the stance, and crouch to lower the body's center of gravity.

Figure 102. Bend knees to absorb waves

Figure 103. Spread skis and bend knees for stability

Just as when getting up, skiers will find that their momentum may make them ski faster than the boat is moving, so the line will exhibit what is referred to as **tow line slack**. Slack in the tow line means that the line is not taut between the skier and boat; in other words, the line is drooping rather than taut. In fact, the line may, on occasion, dip into the water between the boat and skier, should there be a large enough difference between the skier's speed and the boat's speed. In the first case, where the line merely droops, the Advanced Skier can simply hold his or her body position and "take up the slack" with his or her arms by pulling the handle into

Figure 104. Shift weight to turn

the chest. In the second case, where the line actually dips into the water, the skier can expect the line to produce a sudden jerk when the boat pulls the line taut. To prepare for the sudden jerk, the skier should bend knees and arms. Bending the knees will lower the body's center of gravity, and bending the arms will keep the jerk-induced strain isolated in the arm muscles rather than exposing the shoulder sockets to the sudden pulling force. Of course, the skier can simply let the handle go if the jerk is anticipated to be too much to handle. With increasing experience of skier, driver, and spotter, the scenario that created slack in the line will rarely occur. If the problem of tow line slack persists, it may be an indication that the tow line is too long and should be shortened.

The **shoot-across** refers to the case of using the boat's turning to shoot across the wake. To perform the shoot-across, the skier will start on the inside of a turn, then in mid-turn, the skier will angle his or her skis and lean toward the outside of the boat's turning direction. The result is acceleration and speed as we shoot across the wake! Another result is the small jump while crossing each crest.

Figure 105. Crossing wake during turn

Figure 106. Hold stance during faster wake crosses

Figure 107. Shooting across the wake

The next skill with which an Advanced Skier should become familiar is skiing fast-and-wide. To ski **fast-and-wide**, the Advanced Skier will begin to the port or starboard of the wake, then lean outward and use the outside ski edges to propel him or herself farther outside the wake. Getting low will accentuate the move so that the skier gets as close to skiing directly to the side of the straight-course traveling boat as physics will allow. Note that pulling up suddenly will create the type of tow line slack situation that could cause tow line slack. Also, as with all waterskiing skills, skiing fast and wide should be rehearsed on both port and starboard.

Figure 108. *Start outside the wake*

Figure 109. *Lean to get farther out*

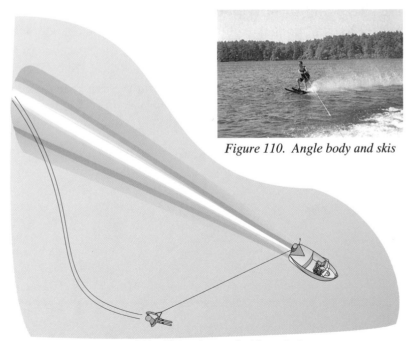

Figure 110. *Angle body and skis*

Figure 111. *Skiing fast and wide technique*

61

Figure 112. Hold tight while boat turns

Figure 113. Getting more aggressive

The **sweep-and-shoot crest-cross** involves speed, timing, and balance by combining the shoot-across, skiing fast-and-wide, and cutback skills. The Advanced Skier will start on the inside of a turn, then shoot across the wake and continue outward by using the skiing fast and wide lean. At the point the driver begins to

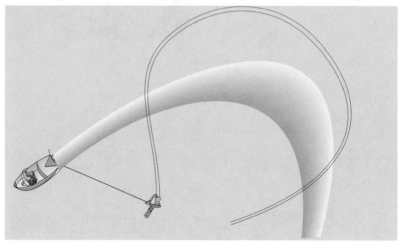

Figure 114. Sweep-and-shoot crest cross maneuver

straighten the boat's course, the skier will then cut back, or shift his or her weight and skis' angles, to the opposite side of the wake and not change this position until shooting across both crests, enjoying the jumps as each crest is crossed. By beginning the cut back when the boat begins its straight line course again, the line will have a slight amount of slack, and thus, the skier will accelerate toward the wake when the tow line slack taken up by the boat's new forward course. The skier can sometimes jump from one crest to the other using this move, if it is performed aggressively enough. The sweep and shoot crest-cross is an advanced skill that takes time to achieve because of the many skills and confidence builders required to develop during the learning stages of waterskiing.

Figure 115. Reduce inside ski pressure

Figure 116. Prepare to cross wake

Figure 117. Crossing wake - knees bent

Figure 118. Crossing the wake

Figure 119. Exiting the wake

On cold days, in an effort to stay warm, experienced tandem skiers may choose to perform a **dock start** so as not to get wet. The trick to a successful dock start is to leave just enough slack in the line to enable the boat to gain enough speed to support the skier's weight immediately, but not so much speed that the tow line's initial tug is too great for the skier to handle or causes harm to the skier's shoulders. Three spread-arm lengths of line coiled in the water is a good length of slack with which to start.

Figure 120. Dock start - 3 coils of slack line

Before starting, the skier puts the skis on and gets a sufficient amount of tow line to make three large coils of line. These coils are then dropped into the water immediately in front of the skier. The skier then slides to the edge of the dock directly behind the motorboat. The skier calls, "Take up the slack!" to the driver, who then puts the engine in forward. When the first of the three coils begins to uncoil as the boat goes forward, the skier calls "Hit it!", whereupon the driver goes to full forward throttle. All the good habits learned during the deep water start exercises should be transferred to the dock start. If the skier sinks into the water,

Figure 121. Dock start take off

64

more line slack should be used on the next attempt. If the skier gets pulled forward or cannot maintain a grip on the handle, less line-slack should be left in the water. The skier must be careful to keep arms bent to allow the muscles, rather than shoulder joints, to take the initial jerk so as not to injure a shoulder. With some practice, dock starts will become as natural as deep water starts.

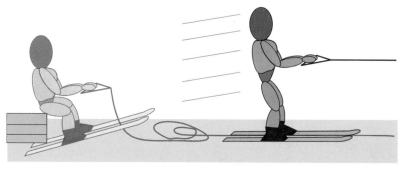

Figure 122. Dock start side view

Now that we are comfortable with tandem ski waterskiing, we are ready to train for slalom skiing. We will use the skier salute drill to get comfortable with standing on one ski.

The **skier salute** is performed by simply lifting one ski and balancing on the other. The ski that the skier raises is the one without the rear boot, into which the dropped-ski foot will be inserted when slalom skiing. Generally, a right-handed individual will tend to place his or her right foot in the slalom ski's rear boot, so, if you are right handed, you will likely practice lifting your

Figure 123. Skier's salute

right ski off the water during the skier salute drill. Likewise, left-handed individuals may choose to lift the left ski off the water during the skier salute drill. If unsure which foot to place in the rear boot, practice raising each foot in turn. If standing on the left leg makes you feel more stable, that is an indication that the right foot should be placed in the rear boot, so the right foot's ski is the one that will later be dropped.

One gets started with the skier salute by lifting the ski off the water for a few feet. At the completion of the drill, however, the skier must be able to ski for more than 100 yards (90 meters) on just one ski. The reason for becoming so proficient at standing on one ski is that we will be dropping one ski and placing the dropped-ski foot in the rear boot of the slalom ski, which means we will be standing on a single ski for a period of time during the transition.

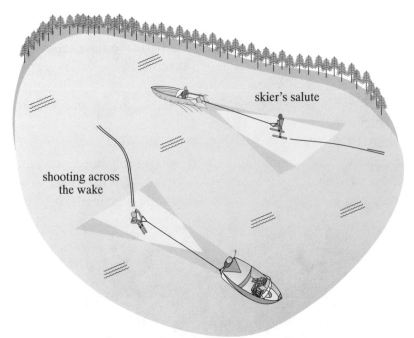

skier's salute

shooting across
the wake

Figure 124. Full tandem ski run with all maneuvers

We have learned and practiced a great deal of waterskiing in the Advanced Skiing section, so let's take a break and learn about and how to use another device people use behind a motorboat, a kneeboard. This activity is known as **kneeboarding**.

One of the big differences between the kneeboarding experience and the waterskiing experience is the wipeout. On waterskis, the wipeout is usually a side, back, or a forward tumble. With all waterski wipeouts, the fall can be anticipated to some extent. On a kneeboard, however, most wipeouts occur when the leading edge of the kneeboard digs beneath the water, which can be very sudden because there is very little distance between the water and one's body when on a kneeboard and because of the rate of rotation of the board and body together. For this reason, we recommend that those with previously injured necks not participate in kneeboarding.

Figure 125. Lean and use edges to turn

The **kneeboard** is a board made of a plastic-like compound, that gives full flotation, and provides padding on the top side, which is shaped for knees. The bottom is designed to enable the kneeboard rider to spin on the water, and make jumps off the wake crests. A kneeboard leg strap with velcro for size adjustment is mounted to the surface of the board to secure the board rider's legs to the board. We recommend operating the motorboat between speeds of 15-25 m.p.h. for kneeboarders, depending on their weight, skill, and experience.

With a little dexterity, the kneeboard rider can push the board beneath the water and slide onto the board. Because of the kneeboard's buoyancy, the kneeboard is a relatively easy flotation device on which to remain balanced. It is also easy to paddle to the tow line.

Figure 126. Swim to reach line

The kneeboard rider prepares for start-up by lying in the water on the kneeboard with the kneeboard's tip out of the water. The tow line is held in one's fingers just over the front tip with thumbs firmly against the board for stability. Once the user is facing the boat and after the slack in the line is taken up by the boat's moving slowly forward, the audible signals used during waterskiing are employed.

Figure 127. Wait for handle

Once ready, the kneeboard user calls, "Hit it!" The boat accelerates slowly, pulling the kneeboard rider, which causes the kneeboard to angle upward, as long as the kneeboard tip remains above the water. While the boat is getting to speed, the kneeboard rider's body is still resting on the kneeboard and his or her legs are extended across the water's surface.

Figure 128. Keep tip up and balance with forearms

When the kneeboard is angled upward (due to water pushing beneath it), the user can brace on his or her elbows on the kneeboard to balance while placing knees onto the kneeboard. Once kneeling upright, the user places the leg strap over his or her thighs. We caution that physically small users have the potential of being held upside down in the water because of the secured strap and the extremely buoyant apparatus, so use discretion before allowing young, small children to use a kneeboard.

Figure 129. Secure thigh strap

Once strapped in, experienced kneeboard users can go outside the wake by leaning and can jump off the water by using the boat's wake crests, and can even do a 360° turn. The trick to performing all these acrobatics is to keep the leading edge angled upward, thereby forcing water beneath the board; if water climbs over the leading edge of the kneeboard, the board will dive into the water, bringing the kneeboard rider in with it, which, as one can imagine, tends to be a very sudden stop.

Once strapped into a kneeboard, the kneeboard rider can go outside the wake by leaning in the direction he or she wishes to travel, which has the effect of using the kneeboard's edge to enable directional control. One of the favorite tricks kneeboard riders like to perform is **riding the large wake crest** that develops during start-up. Balancing on a crest will help develop control over the board's position behind the boat. This position control will be needed in all kneeboard exercises and skills.

Figure 130. Kneeboard surfing

Another trick kneeboard riders perform to demonstrate their skill is the famous 360 degree spin, or simply three-sixty. The key to a successful **three-sixty** is concentrating on keeping the leading edge angled upward, where the leading edge of the kneeboard is always the edge of the board closest to the motorboat, which defines the direction of travel. When a kneeboard rider gets very good at performing three-sixties, they quickly learn that continuously spinning clockwise and counterclockwise can be fast, fun, and entertaining to those on the boat.

Figure 131. 360° leading edge up

Figure 132. 360° - half way around

Figure 133. 360° - complete keeping leading edge up

Besides the hand signals we have learned specifically for skier-spotter communication, the old fashioned "Let's go there!" signal is always effective.

Figure 134. "Let's go there!" hand signal

Kneeboard riders can perform all the same maneuvers as water-skiers, namely the shoot-across, skiing fast-and-wide, and the sweep-and-shoot crest-cross. The difference is that most kneeboards are not designed to allow the sharp cuts one can achieve on waterskis. Nevertheless, a kneeboard rider's speeds and jumps can create some exciting moments!

Figure 135. Flying high

Advanced Review

1. **Wetsuit**. Wetsuits keep waterskiers warm. How does the wetsuit keep a waterskier warm if it allows cold water between it and the skier?

2. **Tow line**. A tow line handle can be swung over the water and released, pulling the tow line as it goes. (a) When later bringing the line into the boat, what can we do to avoid tangles and knots from forming in the line? (b) Where is the tow line handle placed relative to the line?

3. **Driver/Spotter/Skier Responsibilities**. We discussed the safety responsibilities of the driver, spotter, and waterskier while a person is waterskiing. During a pre-ski waterway scouting, what are some obstructions we might observe and stay clear of while towing a skier?

4. **Overboard person**. What equipment might a person on a boat have available to extend to an overboard person or drowning victim so as to stay safely on the boat and out of the victim's reach?

6. **Injured Skier**. An injured waterskier should be moved as little as possible to avoid aggravating or making permanent a neck or back injury. This means that a backboard may need to be floated underwater up to the victim. What should be done to the victim's head and neck once on the backboard?

7. **Crossing Waves**. Besides crossing a wake crest, we are often faced with the challenge of crossing waves from the wake of another motorboat. The larger the waves we must ski over, the more we should bend our (arms / knees / back). (choose the correct choice).

8. **Dock Start**. (a) How many spread-arm lengths of line are recommended to be placed in the water when making a first dock start attempt? (b) If we sink into the water after leaving the dock, should we *increase* or *decrease* the length of line in the water? Why?

9. **Skier Salute**. The skier salute is performed to prepare a skier for dropping a ski to begin slalom skiing. The recommended distance to achieve before the completion of the skier salute is 100 yards (90 meters). To prevent the ski from accidentally being pulled off one's foot by contacting the water, skiers should be conscious to raise high the _____ of the ski.

10. **Kneeboarding**. A kneeboard allows the kneeboard rider to spin 360 degrees, turning backward to the direction of travel in the process of spinning. What must the kneeboard rider do to avoid a wipeout?

Bonus: Perform a shoot-across, fast-and-wide, and sweep-and-shoot crest-cross.

We're now another step along toward Getting off the Ground!

Driver Tools

- **boat bumpers**
- **anchors**
- **fire extinguisher**
- **boat lights**
- **boat horn**

- **bilge pump**
- **battery**
- **propeller types**
- **using a trailer**

In the Beginner and Advanced Tandem Sections, we learned waterskiing skills and some of the responsibilities of the spotter and skier. In the Driver section, we will be learning boat maintenance, fuel handling, and other responsibilities that are needed to maintain and operate the craft. Finally, we will be learning driving skills that will allow us to steer the craft throughout all phases of a normal day of waterskiing.

Figure 136. Tubular boat bumper

Let's start with devices found on and around the boat that are used to keep the craft in good condition. **Boat bumpers**, often shaped like tubes, are recommended to protect the sides of the boat while at a dock or alongside another craft. Boat bumpers can be tied to the boat with 1/8" nylon or dacron line using a bowline or cleat hitch. Once underway, drivers instruct the crew to hang the bumpers inside the boat to keep the boat bumpers from dragging in the water. Boat bumpers are recommended equipment to keep the boat looking aesthetically pleasing and to keep it from being damaged by slow-speed collisions with docks.

Anchors are highly recommended items of safety equipment to protect the boat from potential damage in the event of mishap. Consider the case of losing engine power and being in a strong waterway current leading toward a rocky shore. To stop the boat from being damaged on the rocks, we would use an anchor. The anchor is usually attached to the boat via a 1/2 inch diameter, 3-braid nylon line, or larger, depending on the weight of the boat and the expected waterway currents. Anchors must be sized correctly for the boat, meaning the larger the boat, the larger the anchor and connecting line must be. The shackles, chain, thimbles, line, and other hardware must be scaled accordingly. Before buying such

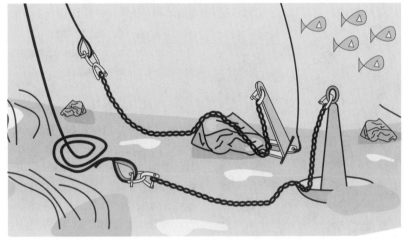

Figure 137. Danforth and mushroom anchor lines

materials or any pre-made anchor assembly, cautious Drivers check to be sure the anchor and other materials are correctly rated for the boat size, waterway bottom, waterway current conditions, and expected wave conditions, if any. Furthermore, the length of the line should be approximately five to ten times the depth of the water to allow the anchor to operate as designed. The chain should be heavy and several feet long to take the small perturbations created by the motion of the floating boat.

Two popular anchor types are the mushroom and Danforth anchors. The **mushroom anchor** looks like an upside-down mushroom and likes muddy bottoms where the base can get beneath the mud and use suction force to provide additional holding power.

The **Danforth anchor** is identified as a flat bar connected to two spades, which works well in most waterway bottom conditions. The spades will trap themselves beneath rocks or burrow their way into sand and mud. A **trip line** floated to the water's surface with a small buoy should be attached to allow dislodging the spades from beneath whatever they have dug themselves.

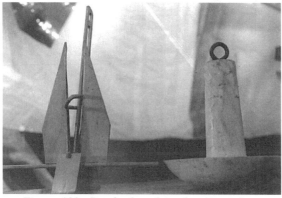

Figure 138. Danforth and mushroom anchors

The most important piece of required safety equipment to have on a motorboat at all times is a **fire extinguisher**. Fires can occur in engines due to an oil or fuel leak, combined with the heat generated on metal parts in the engine. A fire extinguisher appropriate for engine fires is a Class C fire extinguisher, which sprays chemicals that will neither react with nor spread the burning oil as a water-type extinguisher would. Halon gas extinguishers that purge oxygen from the area of the fire are effective since oxygen is required for a fire to continue burning. Halon gas is popular because it does not leave chemical residue; however, one should never spray a Halon extinguisher while standing in a confined space since the oxygen required to breathe will be purged, as well.

Figure 139. Fire extinguisher

Boat lights are required whenever operating on the water between dusk and dawn. There are two boat lights located on a powerboat under twenty-six feet. The first light we will look at is the light found at the bow. Often, there is a single light bulb located inside a fixture having two translucent lenses: one red lens and one green

Figure 140. Bow night lights

lens. When approaching a boat head-on that is using its lights, the red light can be seen on the approaching boat's port side and green light can be seen on the approaching boat's starboard. The classical phrase for remembering the color scheme is "Red-Right-Return," which arises from the traditional concept of staying to the right of the red buoy markers when returning from the open sea. Thus, the red light will indicate

Figure 141. Night lights in action

the side to which to pass the oncoming boat. The second light found on a powerboat is typically a single bright white bulb protected by a clear or opaque lens. During daytime hours, one would not believe these lights offer much safety, but on a clear night, these lights can be seen from a long distance across the water.

Another interesting instrument powered by the boat's electrical system is a boat horn, our audible signal. The control for the boat horn should be located in a convenient location for the driver. Before driving any craft, good Drivers will sound the horn to gain a sense for its volume. This gives a determination of whether an additional airhorn is required aboard the boat, should help from across the waterway be necessary.

A **bilge pump** is used to expel water from the boat. Some bilge pumps are hand cranked, where a piston is run up and down a pipe having an input port and output port. Other bilge pumps use electricity as the power source to suck and blow the bilge water. To engage electric bilge pumps, the boat could have a manual switch, or the pump could have a flotation switch that engages as the water level rises to a certain level, making it an automatic bilge pump. Water is pumped through a hose and back into the waterway.

Figure 142. Bilge pump

Figure 143. Bilge expelling water

The **battery** which must always be protected from water by a battery case, is the heart of the electrical system. The battery gets recharged by the engine when it is running, exactly as does a car battery. And, just as with a car battery, operating any electrical equipment (such as boat lights or an automatic bilge pump) for an extended period of time without operating the engine will reduce the batteries' energy level. Reducing the energy in the battery too much will result in not being able to

Figure 144. Battery inside case

start the engine, because starting the engine requires a great deal of energy from the battery. All electrical wires should be checked occasionally to be sure the insulation is in good condition. Observing any bare wire is cause for replacement of the insulated wire. Also, electrical wires, cables, and terminal blocks must be kept out of the water to avoid "shorting out" the battery, a condition that will at best drain the battery's energy, and at worst cause a fire.

Figure 145. Close and strap down battery case

A **propeller**, a hub with revolving blades that drives a craft, has a noticeable affect on boat performance. **Propeller pitch** is the degree of slope of the propeller blades. High propeller pitch will help the boat to accelerate out of the hole quickly but will reduce its top speed. Waterskiers usually like the boat to accelerate out of the hole quickly to enable them to plane on the water as quickly as possible. Slow acceleration will cause the waterskier to spend energy while dragging through the water waiting for the boat to reach planing speed. Lower propeller pitch will not provide high acceleration out of the hole but may provide a slightly higher top speed.

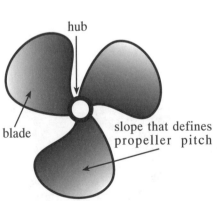

Figure 146. Propeller front view

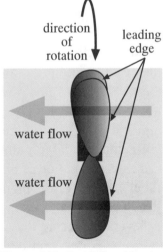

Figure 147. Propeller side view

Propellers make a big difference in engine performance, which is why careful motorboat owners accelerate slowly near the shore so as not to cause the stern to lower (as the bow raises) and strike the waterway bottom, thus damaging the propeller. The material from which a propeller is made matters if we are going to use the boat on the ocean, because the salt in ocean water enables a chemical reaction with many metals, causing corrosion, which weakens their structure and ultimately can cause a catastrophic failure. Two popular and durable **propeller materials** are stainless steel and brass.

A **boat trailer** is used to transport a motorboat. Most boat trailers have boat rollers that allow the boat to roll up the trailer and a **winch** (hand crank). Connecting the winch cable to the bow eyebolt and cranking the winch pulls the boat onto the trailer. Once loaded, the boat winch locks, and straps can secure the boat. A good method is to have one person "reeling" the boat onto the boat trailer using the winch while one or more persons push the boat's transom. The winch cable or line should be checked at regular intervals for fraying and wearing. If the trailer is to be taken on a public road, it must have rear turn signals and stop lights to indicate turning and stopping to other vehicles. Also, the connection to the hauling vehicle must be sufficient to handle the load of the trailer and boat, and the hauling vehicle's engine and brakes must be able to handle the combined load under all foreseeable road conditions.

Figure 148. Loading motorboat onto trailer

Driving with a boat trailer is a skill that needs to be developed through practice. Drivers will find that backing up with a boat trailer should be done slowly and carefully to prevent the trailer from "jackknifing". We recommend speaking with experienced trailer drivers for tips when driving with a boat trailer.

Driver Practical

- environmental care
- fuel storage
- handling fuel
- mixing & carrying fuel
- passing fuel into the craft
- connecting the fuel line

An important goal of all boaters should be maintaining and **protecting the environment**. Since fuel released into the ground and water is toxic to humans, animals, fish, and plant life, and pollutes groundwater, we should take every precaution to prevent fuel from entering the environment. One very easy, inexpensive step is to mix the fuel over a large rubber tray, taking care to properly dispose of any small spillage.

Figure 149. Protect the environment

Fuel storage is an important consideration. One should be sure to keep the fuel shed properly ventilated to prevent fuel vapor buildup. The fuel shed should be free of metal objects that could cause a spark. Because children may not understand the safety hazards of fuel, cautious boaters always return all tanks, cans, and fuel accessories to the ventilated storage facility and lock the door.

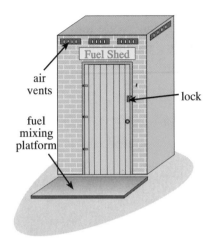

Figure 150. Locked ventilated fuel shed

When **handling fuel**, be sure to avoid getting it on your skin because skin is not impermeable to gasoline; therefore, quickly wash any gas off your skin in case of an accidental splash. Even more important is keeping all fuel products out of eyes, breathing passages, and digestive system. In the event fuel gets in one's eyes, the eyes should be flushed immediately with water, from the tear ducts outward. Medical care should be sought as soon as possible in the event fuel gets in the eyes or is ingested in any way.

Figure 151. Flushing eye with water

Some outboard engines do not have internal engine oil lubrication systems, so boaters will be required to mix gasoline with motorboat engine oil. The motorboat engine oil is used to lubricate the engine pistons. The ratio of gas to oil is usually expressed in gallons to pints; for example, a 5:1 ratio would indicate five gallons of gasoline to one pint of oil. A **fuel mixture** that does not have enough oil or has the wrong type of oil can cause the engine parts to wear out prematurely or become damaged, and a mixture that has an excess amount of oil can cause the spark plugs to foul. Engine manufacturers provide the exact specifications of the

mixture required. To help the oil mix with the gas, a large funnel with a filter screen in the narrow neck is used, where the oil is poured into the funnel at the same time as the gas to help thin the oil and begin the mixing process.

Figure 152. Mixing gas and oil

After the gas and oil are poured into the mixing tank and the **mixing tank** is shaken, the fuel mixture is poured into the **engine fuel tank**. The engine tank can then be carried by one or two persons to the boat.

If the gas and oil were poured into an intermediate mixing tank, the fuel mixture should be poured into the engine fuel tank through a screen filter to prevent any sand and debris from entering the engine. Note that the fuel mixing and transfers are done in a place appro-

Figure 153. Carrying gasoline from fuel shed

priate for such activities, which is not on the boat or near water. Ideally, the ground at the fuel mixing location should be lined with gas- and oil-impermeable materials. The engine fuel tank can then be carried to the boat by one or two persons, if heavy.

When loading the engine fuel tank onto the craft, experienced drivers understand that the weight of a full fuel tank makes teamwork important to prevent unnecessary back strain. One person on the dock lifts the tank for the person in the boat, who will set the tank on the deck. As with raising or lowering any heavy weight, the lifter's back should be kept straight while bending the knees to let the legs do the work.

Figure 154. Passing fuel tank on board

The **engine fuel connection system** is one of two types: twist & lock or poke & click. The engine connection system will define which type of fuel tank connection system is needed. That is, the engine connection system and fuel tank connection systems should both be twist & lock or poke & click so that a standard fuel hose (sometimes referred to as the fuel line) having the same mating connections on each end, can be purchased. When the fuel line connectors are the right mates for the fittings on the engine and fuel tank, attaching a fuel tank via the fuel line to the engine is a very straightforward process. Also, a fuel line is often kept on the boat when not in use, to keep the connectors and line free of sand and debris. This is critical to protect the engine.

Figure 155. Connecting fuel line to fuel tank

Driver Skills

- starting the engine
- leaving the dock
- scouting the waterway
- Rules of the Road
- boat trim
- center of gravity/buoyancy

- docking and beaching
- driving with the tow line
- getting the line to a skier
- pulling up a skier
- driving with a skier
- returning for a skier

In the Beginner and Advanced sections, we learned how to be effective spotters who can communicate to the skier and driver, and we were told that the Driver's responsibilities included getting the tow line to the skier, keeping attention forward when driving for a skier, being aware of other boats and obstructions on the waterway, and knowing where a skier is in relation to the craft before beginning a turn to port or starboard. In the Driver Skills section, we will learn and practice all of these Driver Skills as well as other skills that will allow us to operate and drive the craft for a waterskiing group throughout a normal day on the water. *Note: it is recommended that only persons with a state-issued motor vehicle driver's license be allowed to drive a motorboat.*

As Drivers, one of our first tasks for the day will be **starting the engine**. If it is the first time the motorboat is used in the day, the engine will likely be rotated into 'run' position, which means that the lower end of the engine where the propeller is located must be set into the water. Most engines have a locking mechanism for the 'up-position' that must be released before the engine can be rotated. Once lowered, we should set the 'run-position' locking mechanism to prevent the engine from kicking up while it is in reverse, which happens because the propeller actually climbs backward and rotates the engine until the propeller is out of the water. Engines that have power trim control will not experience

engine in
raised position

rotate engine to
run position

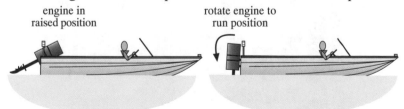

Figure 156. Rotate engine from raised to run position

the reverse-climb effect because the climbing angle force will not be greater than the force the power trim hydraulics exert downward on the engine.

Once the engine is in position and the fuel line has been properly connected, our next task as Drivers will be to perform what is known as **priming the engine**. All standard fuel hoses are equipped with a priming bulb, which is used to begin the fuel siphoning process for the engine. When priming the engine, one squeezes and releases the priming bulb slowly and several times until the bulb is firm, which is the indication that the fuel line is sufficiently full of fuel.

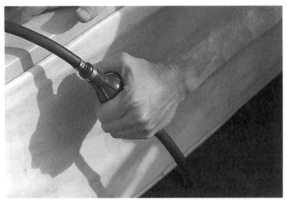

Figure 157. Squeezing bulb to prime fuel line

Over-priming can "flood the engine" which will prevent the engine from starting. In the case of **flooding the engine**, a Driver will have to wait several minutes before the engine will start. After the fuel line is "primed", the fuel line will not need to be primed again while it is attached to both the fuel tank and engine, so long as there is enough fuel in the fuel tank to keep air from entering the fuel line.

Many engines using an external fuel tank may require the Driver to perform an extra step with the fuel tank cap to prevent the engine from stalling while it is operating, namely twisting it into the 'air entry' position to allow air to enter the fuel tank. To burn fuel, the engine combines the fuel liquid with air. If new air is not allowed to enter the fuel tank because the fuel tank cap is sealed "air tight," the engine will exhaust the limited air initially in the sealed fuel tank and the engine will no longer be capable of burning the fuel to produce propeller rotation. One will recognize this problem by first noticing the running engine sounding different from normal and eventually stalling, appearing as though the boat has run out of fuel, even though there is a full tank. If this situation occurs, simply put the fuel tank cap into the "air entry" position, and restart the engine.

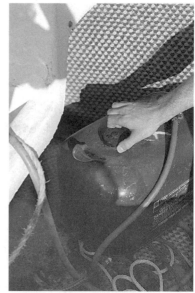

Figure 158. "Air entry" cap adjust

CHECKLIST FOR PREPARING TO START THE ENGINE

1. Lower the engine so the propeller and water (coolant) intake opening are submerged.
2. Set the engine lock mechanism in the 'run' position (to prevent the engine from rising while moving in reverse).
3. Check that the fuel tank has sufficient fuel for the expected driving time and usage.
4. Check that the fuel tank air entry cap or valve mechanism is properly set for air flow.
5. Ensure the fuel hose connectors are mated properly to the engine and fuel tank.
6. Prime the fuel hose.
7. Stow the fuel tank.

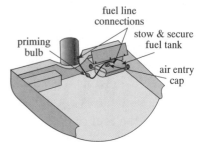

Figure 159. Fuel system configuration

The first time the engine is started each day is slightly different from other times because the engine is "cold", which means the engine may need help from the driver to get started. Help in this case means making engine choke and idle adjustments. If the engine fails to start on one or two successive attempts, a Driver can "choke" the engine. **Choking the engine** means increasing the fuel to air ratio while starting the engine. A popular mechanism to allow a driver to choke the engine is an insertion key receptacle, where the driver simply pushes the key hole assembly inward while the key is turned. Once the engine starts, the Driver should release the key, which disengages the choke. Quite often the engine will run for a few seconds then stop. In such an event, the Driver should restart the engine without applying choke.

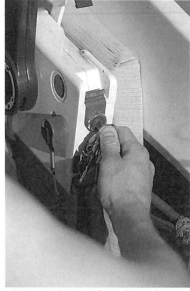

Figure 160. Push and turn key to choke engine during start

The Driver may also find that engine sounds as if it is still too cold or that it is not running strongly enough to start. In such times, the Driver's **raising the engine idle**, by lifting the engine idle lever located on the engine control console, will cause the engine to idle faster. So, when the engine is again attempted to be started, the higher idle speed

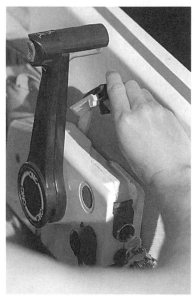

Figure 161. Raise idle lever to assist cold start

will help it stay running. After several seconds, the idle lever should be slowly lowered to the slowest setting. Smoke that is produced by the engine during the choke and raised idle process is normal and will stop after a few moments.

Most motorboat engines used for waterskiing come equipped with an electric start, as opposed to a pull start. When **starting an electric start motor**, the Driver makes sure the throttle lever is in neutral, then turns the ignition key located on the engine control console. Turning the key accesses the battery's power to crank the engine.

Figure 162. Preparing to start the engine

Three things to keep in mind when starting the engine are: choking the engine too long could cause the engine to flood, allowing the engine to idle higher than normal will cause engine wear, and attempting to get the engine to start for too long will drain the battery. A well-tuned engine with a strong battery will start very quickly in most cases. Engines that continually require excessive starting times may need to have spark plugs cleaned or changed, or the engine may need a general tune-up.

Before starting the boat, the boat dock lines should be released and the boat should be facing the open water. The driver should make a last survey of the waters for swimmers and other hazards, check that all crew members are seated and wearing PFDs, then engage the throttle in forward or reverse, depending on which allows the most efficient, yet safest, path available to clear the dock.

Figure 163. Debarking from the dock to avoid creating wakes and for safety

The lever used to control forward, neutral, and reverse motion is called the **throttle**. The boat is always turned on and off in neutral. Neutral is nearly universally set with the throttle lever vertical, in a locked position between forward and reverse. Neutral prevents the propeller from spinning. To start the boat, we simply turn the key, usually clockwise. The boat can be put in forward gear by depressing the throttle-in-neutral locking mechanism (located on the throttle) and rotating the throttle forward. The driver rotates the throttle backward for reverse gear. In forward and reverse gear, or simply forward or reverse, the farther from the neutral position the throttle is rotated, the faster the boat travels forward or backward, respectively.

Figure 164. Throttle in neutral

Figure 165. Throttle in reverse

Figure 166. Throttle in slow speed forward position

Figure 167. Throttle in high speed forward position

When a novice Driver is being introduced to driving a motorboat, a more experienced Driver should bring the craft out into deep water and put the engine in neutral. This allows the novice Driver to get a feel for driving without having to worry about obstacles, such as docks or other boats, often found close to shore.

New Drivers should begin **driving practice** by turning the engine on, putting the boat into forward, slowly bringing the boat to full speed, maintaining a constant speed between 25 m.p.h. and 35 m.p.h. (40 and 57 kilometers per hour), turning left and right, slowing down, then putting the boat back into neutral. The new Driver should also practice putting the boat into reverse and slowly driving backward, remembering that the bow will turn in the opposite direction from that in which the steering wheel is turned. The opposite reaction is due to the propeller pulling the stern toward the direction the propeller is spinning. Again, all engines must have their locking mechanisms engaged so that the engine is secured down while in reverse.

When learning to drive, practicing on a **driving obstacle course** may help in developing boat handling skills. The new Driver may find that simply driving around the perimeter of the waterway and then slowing down to manipulate the boat around rafts or other moored craft located on the waterway will significantly improve the coordination required to handle the motorboat.

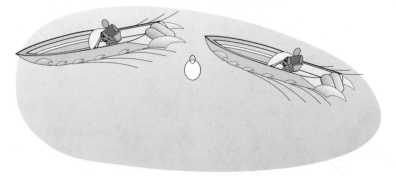

Figure 168. New driver obstacle course for practicing skills

As good Drivers, we must get into the habit of scouting the waterway on a daily basis. **Scouting the waterway** is intended to make the Driver and crew keenly aware of waterway hazards, such as rocks, logs, branches, shallow water, and man-made structures. Changes in waterway obstacles, particularly man-made ones, can occur without notice. The time spent scouting the waterway will give the engine time to warm up, which is important to do before pulling a skier, because pulling up a skier before the engine is warm will put excessive stress on the engine.

Figure 169. Daily waterway scouting

While scouting the waterway, the Driver will likely cross paths with other craft, so the driver should know right-of-way rules for boats, more commonly known as **Rules of the Road**. The situations described below are based upon the Inland Rules. First, less maneuverable craft have right-of-way over more maneuverable craft. That means engineless craft, particularly craft dependent on wind, have right-of-way over small, maneuverable power boats. When encountering another craft nearly head on, the boats should keep to the right, which is the same as the corresponding traffic rule for automobiles. When boats are far to starboard of each other, so as not to be considered meeting head on, the craft should simply continue straight rather than passing to starboard.

In situations where the craft are to cross paths at an angle, the craft on the right has right-of-way, again, similar to the corresponding highway traffic rules, for cars that meet at an unmarked intersection. The craft on the left (the burdened vessel) must make any necessary adjustments to speed or course to pass astern of the privileged craft, allowing it to pass without having to change course or speed. A vessel being overtaken has the right-of-way over overtaking craft. The faster boat may pass the slower boat to starboard or port. If the faster boat wishes to pass to starboard, the Driver should give a single audible blast. The slower vessel should respond with a single audible blast if it is safe to do so. If passing to port is desired, two audible blasts should be made during the exchange. Four or more audible blasts should be made by the slower vessel if it is not safe that he be passed. Remember, a powerboat operator always has the option of throttling down to a stop.

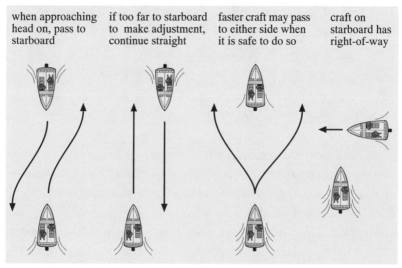

| when approaching head on, pass to starboard | if too far to starboard to make adjustment, continue straight | faster craft may pass to either side when it is safe to do so | craft on starboard has right-of-way |

Figure 170. Rules of the road

The purpose of the Rules of the Road is to prevent accidents by establishing certain procedures that boat operators must follow when danger of collision exists. Under certain conditions, a departure from the rules may be necessary on the part of the vessels involved, to avoid immediate danger. Remember, the **Basic Rule of the Road** is to avoid collisions: this is especially true if you are the smaller of the two craft.

While driving, the motorboat may be seen from the side as bow high, bow low, or boat level. A boat having an improper angle may be felt as **porpoising**, which can cause loss of control. The fore or aft angle of the boat may be created by uneven weight distribution of gear and/ or crew, or by the angle of the engine. For gear or crew causes, either or both should be adjusted fore or aft to make the craft ride level. In the case of engine angle being the cause of the boat angle, drivers having automatic engine trim capability on the boat can adjust the engine angle to correct the boat angle relative to the water's surface. This is referred to as **trimming the hull from bow to stern**. For boats without automatic engine trim capabilities, the angle of the boat as caused by the engine angle must be determined, then the engine is turned off, and the trim pin must be removed, preferably at shore, to adjust the boat trim. If the bow is digging, the engine should be rotated upward away from the transom.

Figure 171. Boat trim, bow "digging"

If the bow is raised, the engine should be rotated downward toward the transom. Bear in mind that boat trim is affected both by weight distribution on the boat and engine angle, so Drivers of lighter craft having automatic trim may make slight adjustments to engine angle as crew members change seat locations.

Figure 172. Boat trim, bow too high

Figure 173. Boat trim, proper trim

Trimming the hull from port to starboard is also important in maintaining control over the craft. Experienced Drivers refer to the hypothetical physical forces involved as "keeping the center of gravity centered over the center of buoyancy" so as to keep the boat level from side to side. The **center of gravity** is the imaginary point where all the forces on the boat could be located and still apply the same downward force on the hull. The **center of buoyancy** is the imaginary point where all the forces resisting the weight of the hull could be centered and still have the same upward buoyancy force on the hull.

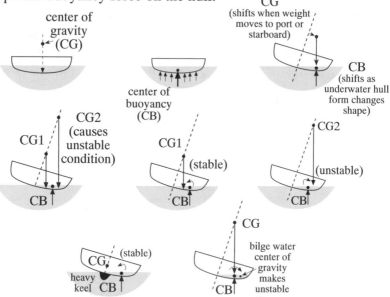

Figure 174. Center of gravity and center of buoyancy

The center of buoyancy must stay beneath the center of gravity or to the outside of the center of gravity during a turn or capsizing may result. The center of gravity could move beyond the center of buoyancy toward the edge of the boat if there is an extreme weight too high on the craft. A high center of gravity will cause the boat to have excessive tilt during turns and could cause the driver to lose control of the boat. *CAUTION: Every motorboat has a maximum loading (weight) rating specified by the manufacturer, meaning that the sum of all gear and passenger weights must be below the rated weight; failure to adhere to the specified weight rating could result in capsizing or sinking the motorboat.*

The last of the non-skier-related Driver Skills we will learn are docking and beaching. In both cases, all crew members should remain seated, with arms and hands inside the craft, until the boat has come to a complete stop. Good driving skills should provide the stopping force.

Docking and patience are synonymous. The Driver puts the throttle in neutral at approximately five boat lengths before the dock. After setting the boat at a 45 degree angle to the near-side of the dock section to where he or she wishes to set the boat parallel, the driver will continue on this 45° approach, toggling the throttle between forward and neutral. The Driver must consider the potential "push" of any waves from behind the motorboat and approach the dock slowly. At one and one-half boat lengths, the driver turns the boat to be nearly parallel to the dock, then drifts in neutral nearly to the dock, remembering to deploy the boat bumpers.

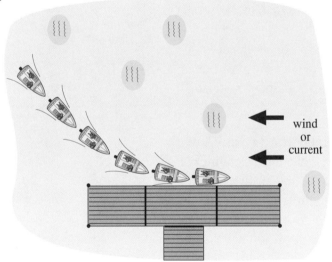

wind
or
current

Figure 175. Docking a boat

Just before reaching the dock, the driver spins the steering wheel (and propeller) toward the dock, then engages the engine in reverse to stop forward momentum and to pull the stern alongside the dock. The throttle is set to neutral position and the docking is completed by cleat-hitching the craft to the dock. When wind or water current is present, the Driver should make the approach such that the bow faces into the wind or water current; note that if the water current has more effect on the boat than the wind, and the water current and wind are from different directions, the Driver should point the bow into the water current when docking. Also, Drivers should be aware that every craft responds differently to slow-speed control, so bad docking approaches are likely. For this reason, it is best to remember that reversing and making a re-approach takes only time, whereas completing a miscalculated approach will cost time and money.

Beaching, like docking, takes patience. A sufficient distance from shore is chosen to set the engine in neutral. The Driver keeps an eye on the water's bottom to determine when to shut the engine off and raise it to prevent damaging the propeller and lowest point of the engine. The final distance to shore is traversed by paddling or hand-towing. Once ashore, the boat is lifted onto the sand (and secured by its bow eyebolt to a heavy block or permanent shore fixture if the craft will remain beached for an appreciable length of time).

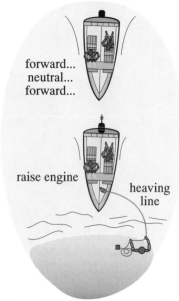

The **end of the day shutdown** includes turning the engine off, disconnecting the fuel line, and raising the engine out of the water. It is recommended that the engine be left with some fuel in its lines by simply turn-

Figure 176. Beaching a motorboat

ing it off, rather than disconnecting the fuel line and letting the engine burn all the remaining fuel inside it, stalling when no more fuel remains. The reason that leaving fuel inside is preferable is that fuel is a lubricant, since it contains the oil mixture. That means the next time the engine is started it will have some internal lubrication rather than starting with little to none, which causes undue wear. The fuel line is disconnected to protect it from having stress placed on it, particularly at the connector/hose joints, when the engine is tilted. Finally, raising the engine will keep it from having biological growth - vegetation from fresh water or barnacles from saltwater - build up on the propeller and water-exposed engine parts while the boat is sitting still. This will keep these parts as maintenance-free as possible.

Figure 177. Raise engine at end of day

Now that we have learned the fundamentals of driving and maintaining a motorboat, we must become proficient at **driving a motorboat for a waterskier**. Before we drive with a skier in tow, we must understand what it means to have a waterskiing tow line behind the boat. First, a driver should think of the boat length as being extended by the length of the tow line, meaning that a far greater space allowance must be given for the line and boat than the boat alone. Next, we must presume that other boats will not be aware of the tow line. For example, if another motorboat's path

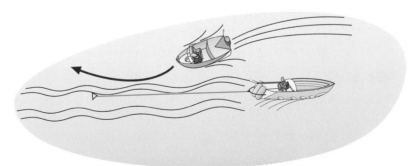

Figure 178. Be aware of tow line length behind boat

is such that it will cross from port to starboard behind the boat having the tow line outstretched, we, as Drivers, should anticipate the potential for other boats to drive over the tow line. To prevent this problem, we could either stop or slow well ahead of time to allow the other motorboat to pass, or we could turn to starboard well ahead of time so the boats' paths do not cross. Since we cannot expect other drivers to see the tow line, especially while we are traveling at slow speeds or at rest, experienced Drivers keep the line in the boat when a skier has completed his or her run.

Another skill a driver needs to have is that of efficiently **getting the tow line to a skier** who will be performing a deep water start. Because a line cannot be pushed, Drivers need to learn to drag the line in a controlled fashion. Remember that the handle tends to resist pulling motion on the line by the boat. By turning the motorboat relative to the handle, we can bring the tow line to the waterskier without the waterskier's having to move.

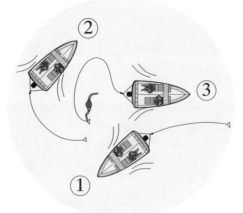

Figure 179. Getting tow line to skier overview

While moving the tow line to the skier, drivers will shift from forward to neutral, moving past the skier in a circle. It is important that the driver always passes the skier off the Driver's side of the craft. So, if the steering wheel is located on starboard, the craft will circle the waterskier such that the waterskier is in the water off starboard, allowing the Driver to see the waterskier the entire time for the safety of the waterskier.

Figure 180. Driver always keeps skier in view

Note that this circling is performed at a very slow speed, and is completed in neutral, with the boat facing the direction the skier will begin skiing. If the tow line does not get to the skier, the driver can repeat the circle, but the skier may simply wish to swim backward a short distance to get the line. The tow line handle is brought to the skier once the tow line is in hand by briefly moving the throttle from forward to neutral until the handle reaches the skier. At this point, the boat should be in neutral, the tow line should be nearly straight between the skier and boat, and the skier should be facing the boat with the line passing between the two skis.

Figure 181. Maintain contact with the tow line for driver

At the start of a skier's run, the **Driver's duties** include: to watch for other boats, position the boat directly in front of the skier, and to accelerate the craft in a manner that aids the skier's successful start.

Figure 182. Show handle to spotter

Watching for other boats means to watch for boats or other objects immediately to the front or sides of the craft and to watch for moving boats that could interfere with the skier's path. The general rule regarding starts is to *wait until all other craft have passed* rather than to try to hurry before them. Although the skier will have to contend with the wake from the passing motorboat, the alternative is to place the skier in harm's way.

The next duty the Driver has is to position the boat directly in front of, and facing away from, the skier. This positioning will most effectively give the skier a fast and straight pickup. The driver should generally try to face the boat directly into the wind and/or current for skier start-up. Windy days tend to push the boat downwind of the skier and force the driver to correct the position of the boat for skier start-up.

The Driver's last duty at the start of the skier's run is **driving for a deep water start**. For a deep water start, the skier has two choices: full throttle or smooth acceleration. The Driver should ask the skier his or her preference. Generally, heavier craft accelerate slowly out of the hole, so immediate full throttle may be fine for a skier. Lighter boats with powerful engines may overpower a new skier, so the driver may need to perform a slower, smoother acceleration.

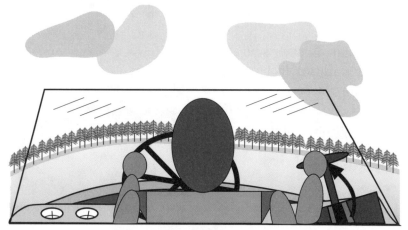

Figure 183. When starting, adjust acceleration for skier ability

When performing a **full throttle acceleration**, the driver will wait for the skier's "Take up the slack!" signal, then take up the slack in the line by moving the throttle from neutral to forward gear at the slowest setting. Once the slack has been taken up, the skier will call "Hit it!", then the driver "guns it" by quickly rotating the throttle forward to the full speed setting. Depending on the motorboat's start-up characteristics and bow design, the driver may need to put him or herself into a position to see over the bow should it raise up during full throttle acceleration.

When performing a **smooth acceleration**, the Driver will again take up the slack, then, after the "Hit it!" signal, the Driver will slowly rotate the throttle to the full acceleration position. Smooth accelerations allow the skier to find his or her balance while getting up.

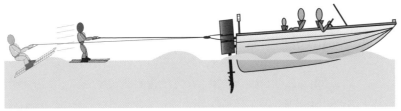

Figure 184. Drag pickup to give beginner skier stability before fast pickup

In addition to watching for boats that may interfere before starting a skier, Drivers should consider the **water depth** with respect to the propeller; that is, when the bow raises, the stern lowers. Striking the bottom can irreparably damage the engine shaft and propeller, which are expensive to repair and replace.

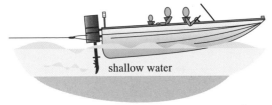

shallow water

Figure 185. Propeller goes deeper when accelerating

After successfully pulling up the skier, the Driver is responsible for **choosing the skier's path**. The Driver selects the general pattern and distance from the natural boundaries of the waterway, as well as the distance from natural and man-made obstructions, other craft, and swimmers.

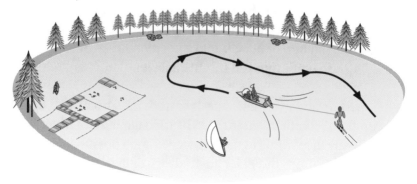

Figure 186. Pre-chosen course to pull the skier

The general waterski driving course the Driver should plan is usually based on the skier's experience and expertise. Novice skiers will often require long straight paths with wide turns, and more experienced skiers might prefer shorter straight paths with tight turns to stay in a very smooth section of water protected from the wind by a tree lined area of the shoreline. The Driver must also take into account the depth of the water and general boat traffic when planning and driving the general waterskiing course. The Driver should discuss the projected course with the skier before he or she enters the water. Additionally, if either Driver or skier has never traveled the planned general course, both should drive it to learn its characteristics.

The Driver may also be required to make real time decisions on the detailed path while underway. For instance, a canoe may have entered the waterway and blocked the expected path. The Driver can choose to pass the canoe to the starboard or port, but, passing the canoe on starboard may put the motorboat and skier too close to shore, so the Driver will be forced to pass the canoe on port. Another case could be crossing paths with another motorboat, maybe even one towing a skier. The Driver should know at all times the location of all other craft in the area so as not to be unpleasantly surprised. Remember, stopping the motorboat is always a better option than trying to "make it," but, as good Drivers, we should be aware of other craft so that those are not our only choices.

When making both the general and real-time course decisions, Drivers must also consider the skier's position relative to the course change. Generally, if the skier is outside the port wake, the Driver should not turn to port because the tow line will slacken, potentially causing the skier to lose speed and begin to lower into the water. When the skier begins to sink into the water, the tow line will jerk him or her forward when the slack is taken up again. If the Driver can wait until the skier is in the wake or on the outside of the wake with respect to the direction of turn, the driver should opt to wait.

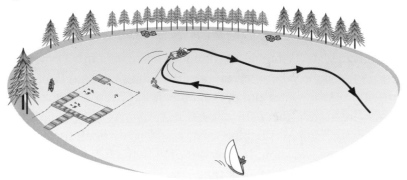

Figure 187. Turning away from the skier

If the skier understands how to compensate for turning if caught on the inside of the wake, the driver can begin a slow turn. Remember, the spotter should communicate the Driver's intention to the skier by using the predetermined signals. If there is not enough time to wait for the skier to get into a good position to handle a turn before turning is required, the Driver may be forced to choose from the last options: slowing the craft to give the skier time, or stopping. Remember, the Driver is ultimately responsible for the safety of the skier while he or she in tow.

Whenever a skier falls or intentionally releases the handle, the Driver's responsibility becomes one of boat control (for **retrieving the skier** as quickly and safely as possible). A good method is to decelerate, turn, then re-accelerate back to the skier. Before slowing, the Driver should be sure the passengers are all seated to avoid throwing them around the cockpit. The craft should be slowed approximately five boat lengths away from the skier unless there is an emergency.

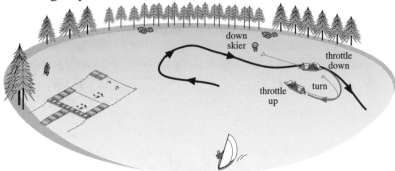

Figure 188. Reacting to a fallen or "released" skier

The day of waterskiing should be ended when the sun becomes too low in the sky. When **driving at dusk**, the sun can reflect very brightly off the water and prevent the driver from looking in the sun's direction. Other parts of the waterway may be very dark and other craft, such as a fishing boat, could be difficult to see. As good Drivers, we should know our time limits for towing skiers, use our safety lights at dusk (and later), and drive slowly on the waterway when lighting is poor.

Figure 189. Watch for other craft at dusk

Driver Review

1. **Boat Anchors**. A boat anchor can protect the hull by keeping the boat on the water safely away from rocks on the shoreline. Can you name a boat anchor type and describe its distinguishing characteristics?

2. **Fire Extinguisher**. Motorboats are required to carry working fire extinguisher capable of extinguishing oil and fuel fires. We discussed how chemical and Halon gas Type C extinguishers put out oil and fuel fire. Why does a reasonably prudent Driver not simply throw water on such a fire?

3. **Electrical Equipment**. What happens to a boat battery if the lights are left on or the bilge pump continuously runs without the engine being turned on for a long period of time?

4. **Fuel Storage**. List some guidelines when storing gasoline and oil.

5. **Fuel Handling**. If gasoline gets on one's skin, the skin should be washed with soap and water. (a) What should one do if gasoline gets in one's eye? (b) What about if someone ingests (swallows) gasoline?

6. **Fuel Line**. Mixing gasoline and oil in their specified amounts should be done in a sand-free area, and sand filters should be used on funnels designed for this purpose. The fuel line should be kept on the boat, away from sand, when not in use. What is the problem with getting sand in the fuel or fuel line?

7. **Starting the Engine**. What two controls can be adjusted when starting a cold motorboat engine?

8. **Driving in Forward and Reverse**. We learned how to drive a boat in forward and reverse. (a) What direction does the bow turn when driving forward and turning the steering wheel toward port? (b) What direction does the bow turn when in reverse and turning the steering wheel toward port?

9. **Driving for a Skier**. To get the tow line to a skier preparing to perform a deep water start, the Driver is responsible for getting the tow line to the skier. (a) Can you list some Driver duties and tips for making this an easier task? (b) When pulling up an inexperienced skier, what techniques can a Driver use to aid in this effort?

10. **Pulling a Skier**. The driver must watch for obstructions, including other motorboats, while towing a skier to protect the skier and the passengers. What about the skier should a driver know before making a turn to starboard or port?

Bonus: Make three consecutive good docking attempts in a row.

We're now one step away from Getting off the Ground!

Slalom Tools

- line types
- caring for line
- tying an eyesplice
- whipping
- making an anchor
- tossing a heaving line

In the Beginner and Advanced Sections, we learned a lot of nomenclature, communication skills, and skills for tandem water-skiing. In the Slalom Section we will be learning more about lines, nomenclature specific to slalom skiing, and slalom skiing skills.

Line is rope cut for a purpose. The different **line types** often used in boating are: manila, nylon, dacron, and polypropylene. Manila, which is often used for moorings and anchors, costs less than synthetics, but is rough on the hands. Manila line wears from sand and long periods of wetness.

manila

nylon

dacron

polypropylene

Figure 190. Line types

Nylon is a very popular synthetic line because of its strength, flexibility, softness, and resistance to mildew and abrasion. Nylon is good for anchor and mooring lines because its stretch quality provides shock-absorption.

Dacron, another synthetic line, has a low stretch quality and retains full strength when wet. Dacron, like nylon, is flexible, soft, and resistant to mildew and abrasion.

Polypropylene is another low stretch synthetic line, but polypropylene is more susceptible to abrasion than nylon or dacron.

Because polypropylene floats very well, its best use is as a floating line, such as a waterskiing line or mooring pickup.

Line care involves swishing or shaking a line in the water to clean it of sand and other foreign debris. Using a high pressure hose tends to force sand deeper into the line, causing the line to weaken. Sand and other particles weaken line because their microscopic sharp edges wear and cut the small fibers from which a line is made. The best method for maintaining a clean, strong line is by storing it on clean dry surfaces. Today's lines can take a lot of abuse, but regular inspection and replacement of lines that exhibit wear, mildew, or general aging is recommended to keep the tow line, anchor line, mooring lines, and

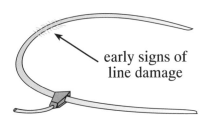

early signs of line damage

Figure 191. Replace frayed lines

dock lines functional and safe. In particular, careful inspection of the tow line and bridle should be performed as a skier could be unexpectedly surprised or injured if the tow line were to break.

Up to this point, we've learned knots and hitches that are used to secure the boat to a dock and to be used generally about the craft. The next two additions to our knot skills, splicing and whipping, are useful in making anchor lines, mooring lines, and dock lines.

To prepare for **splicing**, we first take three pieces of tape, each approximately one loop's worth around the line, and set them aside. Next, take a three braid line - 3/8" nylon is easy to use while learning - and tape in the direction of the rope twist approximately 3" to 6" above the braiding end. This piece of tape will prevent the line from completely unraveling.

3"-6"

Figure 192. Unbraid and tape 3"-6"

107

Now separate the piece of line into its three component strands and tape the three loose ends tightly using the three pieces of tape set aside earlier. Leave a small piece of line showing beyond those pieces of tape so the tape does not slide off the end.

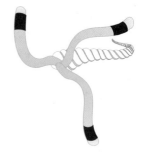

Figure 193. *Separated line*

We are now ready to make the eyesplice. Start with the standing end away from you. Next, take the running end, point it away from you, and lay it on top of the standing end. Your permanent loop size is determined by the loop created by the length of running end folded back onto the standing end. At this point, two of the three component running end strands should be draping over opposite sides of the standing end, with the third lying on top of the standing end.

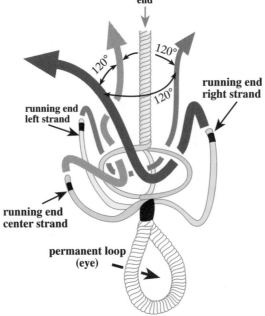

Figure 194. *Eye splice, 1st weave*

To begin the splice, slightly back-twist the standing end to open a gap between the three component strands. Next, take the running end center strand and weave it into the standing end by guiding it through the gap beneath the top standing end strand (which we raised and separated by back-twisting the standing end). Back-twist the standing end and guide the left running end strand through the gap just left of where the center strand came out. Take the right running strand and weave it under the standing end strand not yet on top of a running end strand. Each running end strand should now be 120° apart. Braid over and under in a clockwise fashion (against the natural twist of the standing end line) until a little more than the tape on the running end component strands is showing. Rolling the completed splice between our hands will make the braid smooth.

Figure 195. Completed eye splice

To secure the end of the splice, we can use whipping line. Whipping line is thin and often wax-coated. Let's learn one **whipping** technique. Make a loop on top of the three-braid line with the whipping line. Twist the whipping line running end around the three-braid line, working up the whipping line loop. Put the running end through the loop. Pull the standing end so the loop is beneath the twist. Tie a square knot with the excess running and standing ends of the whipping line. Turn the running and standing ends in opposite directions around the line being whipped, and complete the whip by tying another square knot.

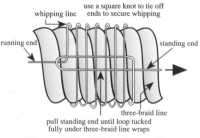

Figure 196. Whipping technique

Let's now look at **how to make an anchor assembly**. Our goal is to have no line exposed to metal because the line will quickly wear. Starting at the anchor, connect the chain to it through the use of a **shackle**. Connect the other end of the chain to the **thimble** (eye-spliced in the line), using another shackle.

Figure 197. Shackle

Figure 198. Thimble

A chain weighing as much as or more than the anchor should be attached between the anchor and line to buffer boat movement from dragging or even picking up the anchor. 1/2" line is thick for small boats but easy to handle. Generally, the anchor line length should be five to ten times the depth of water in which it is used. At the other end of the line from the anchor, we can choose to make an eyesplice loop or splice another thimble into the line so as to attach a clip via a shackle to connect to an eyebolt on the craft. We may also choose to leave the boat end untouched to allow easy tying to a cleat. Many boaters like to have a permanent eyesplice loop on the boat end, and it would be good practice for us to make one. We should use stainless steel, nylon coated, or galvanized metal parts to protect chains, anchors, thimbles, shackles, and other metal parts exposed to water from rusting. Also, if using a Danforth anchor, be sure to attach a buoy to a small trip line that reaches from the anchor to the water's surface to enable retracting the spades from beneath an object under which they may have dug.

Figure 199. Anchor assembly with mushroom anchor

A **monkey's fist** knot is useful for heaving lines and is fun to make. Inside the monkey's fist is a block of wood, which floats.

When **tossing a heaving line** with a money's fist (or other such flotation attached to the heaving line's tossing end), the crew member tossing the line should attempt to place the flotation beyond - rather than short of or at - the receiver. This tossing technique will avoid injury and enable the crew to pull the monkey's fist, which

Figure 200. Monkey's fist knot

floats because of the wood, to the receiver instead of requiring a time consuming re-toss by the crew should the toss be too short.

Figure 201. Tossing rescue line with monkey's fist technique

Slalom Practical

- selecting waterskis
- trim tab
- tow line types
- waterski boom

Since we will soon be slalom waterskiing, we should be familiar with basic **waterski designs** so that we are better able to select skis that match our physical attributes, and skiing abilities, and personal goals. Waterskis can often make a noticeable difference in a skier's level of performance, so let's look at some waterski physical characteristics that affect their handling on the water...

Waterskis come in different lengths and styles. There are very small waterskis with small boots, that weigh significantly less than the skis we've seen. These small skis are meant for children. The shorter, lighter skis allow children to more easily control the skis while putting them on in the water and while skiing.

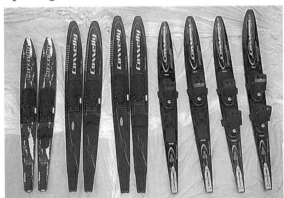

Figure 202. Junior tandem, adult tandem, and adult slalom waterskis

There are also the combination tandem skis we used in the Beginner and Advanced Sections. Combination, or combo, in this context means combination tandem and slalom skis. Combo skis have a half-boot on one of the skis that allows the skier to slide a foot into this half-boot and use the one combo ski for slalom skiing. These tandem skis come in different lengths, usually between 65 inches and 72 inches (165-185 cm). Shorter, thinner skis tend to be less stable, but allow skiers to turn more easily. Longer, wider skis are more stable but do not allow a skier to turn as quickly as the shorter, narrower skis.

The last type of waterskis are the double full-boot slalom skis that strap securely onto both feet. Dedicated, high performance, slalom skis are great for the slalom skier who really wants a ski that will enable smooth, sharp cuts, big rooster tails, and a comfortable ride. Some slalom skis are designed to help the user get on the edges to carve more fluidly through the water. Shorter, narrower slalom skis will allow a skier to make sharper cuts. Some types of tandem and slalom waterskis have a wide **waterski groove** along the bottom centerline of the ski to help the ski stay pointed in the direction the skier wants and to improve cutting performance (i.e., a deeper groove will aid the skier in making a tighter turn).

Figure 203. Ski bottom shape

To help slalom skiers keep the back end of the ski in the water during a cut, Slalom Skiers may choose to attach a **trim tab** to the fin. A trim tab extends horizontally out from the fin approximately one inch (2.54 cm). The trim tab will have water passing

above and below the horizontal tabs, which will hold the back end of the ski on the water, especially while crossing the wake. Sharp cuts will also feel smoother and more stable because of the trim tab.

Figure 204. Ski fin with trim tab

Figure 205. Trim tab rear view

Figure 206. Trim tab holds ski down

Just as waterskis come in different sizes and styles, so are there waterskiing **tow line types**. First, there are different grades of polypropylene line, where some are softer and last longer than others. Next, some tow lines come as a single length, where others are sectionals (i.e., sections can be added or removed). Some lines are multi-color while others are unicolor. There are tow lines specially designed to work with a ski pole, and others that interface only with a traveler on a bridle. The quality of handles vary from hard and round to soft and ergonomically designed. The point is that as Slalom waterskiers, we should be familiar with the various lines available and selective about the type of line we choose to use.

Novice Slalom waterskiers and waterskiers learning to bare-foot can get a lot out of using a **boom** extending to the side of the boat, usually supported by the ski pole. The Slalom waterskier will start in the regular slalom starting position - that will be taught in the Slalom Skiing section - but hold the boom rather than the tow line. When the boat gets up to speed, the Slalom Skier will find that holding the boom will provide excellent support while standing on one ski. After having

Figure 207. Boom for slalom training

gotten used to the sensation of standing on only the slalom waterski, the skier should stop, then begin using the tow line. The tow line will not offer the same lateral support the boom, so one should not expect immediate slalom skiing proficiency when making the transition from a pole to the tow line, but at least standing on one ski will have been experienced.

Slalom Skiing Skills

- dropping a ski
- deep water start
- slalom skiing stance
- leaving the wake
- skiing over waves
- cutting
- advanced arm/hand coordination
- throwing a spray

In the Advanced Skiing Skills Section, we learned to ski on both sides of the wake, control our positions relative to the boat, and cross the wake in the various tandem skiing drills. We also learned to stand on one ski in a drill known as the skier salute. In the Slalom Skiing Skills section, we will learn how to stand on the slalom ski with both feet, move into and out of the wake on one ski, perform the wake crossing drills we learned in the Advanced Skiing section, understand how to spray smooth walls of water, and finish with the whip cut.

Before we begin slalom skiing, we should recall the stretching exercises learned in the Beginner Skiing section. When first learning to waterski, most Beginners find that their legs are stretched or used in ways to which they may not be normally be exposed, such as while putting on the skis or skiing over the wake. The stretching is meant to prevent or lessen effects from the new activity. Likewise, while learning and performing slalom waterskiing, we will find ourselves stretching and using muscles in ways that are not often part of a person's daily routine, such as standing on the slalom ski with one foot immediately in front of the other. Remember, the muscles we should stretch are the quadriceps, hamstrings, and calf muscles in our legs, and also loosen the ankles, feet, back, neck, chest, shoulders, and hands. Because all of the muscles in these locations will contribute to slalom skiing, all are potential candidates to be sore if not adequately stretched before skiing.

Figure 208. Stretch hamstrings and calves

There are two basic methods used to begin slalom waterskiing: dropping a ski or performing a deep water start. When using either method, the foot on which we have found ourselves better able to balance (or felt more comfortable on) during the skier salute drill should be placed in the front boot of the slalom ski. The other foot will be placed in the slalom ski rear boot.

Figure 209. Become confident on slalom ski

Dropping a ski to begin slalom skiing is the first method we will learn since we are now comfortable with standing on one ski by having practiced the skier salute. The skier salute should be practiced again to build confidence before dropping the ski. **Dropping a ski** means to release the to-be rear slalom ski foot from the non-slalom ski and then placing the rear slalom foot into the rear slalom ski boot. To prepare for dropping the ski, the ski boot on the non-slalom ski should be loosened before starting on both skis in a standard tandem ski deep water start. After skiing on both skis, then signaling to the spotter to slow the boat (usually to between 20-30 m.p.h. when first learning this skill) and getting the agreed-to "okay to drop" signal in return, we can go through the steps of releasing the ski.

1. Raise the heel of the non-slalom ski out of the ski boot about to be released.
2. Raise the foot straight up out of the boot, allowing the ski to slowly drift behind.
3. Slowly, yet affirmatively, bring the raised foot to the rear slalom ski boot.
4. Insert the free foot into the slalom ski rear boot.

Figure 210. Lift heel and release ski

Figure 211. Same balance as skier salute

Figure 212. Slide foot into rear boot

Because we are comfortable with standing on the front foot for a long distance, we should be relaxed if unable to find the rear boot immediately with the free foot. The **tree ski** is another drill applicable to the dropping the ski method. To do the tree ski, loop one tow line around a tree (or post) at chest level, place both skis on the ground such that they are not resting on the fins, and go through the ski release procedure we just learned. Once both feet are in the slalom ski boots, we can practice balancing on land in the slalom waterskiing position without worrying about falling.

Figure 213. Tree ski practice method

Standing on one ski will soon become as natural as standing on two skis. The same basic arm and knee bends apply; that is, slightly bent arms will absorb the variations of tow line pull, and slightly bent knees will absorb the turbulence in the wake and waves. Of course, the rest of the body should be kept relaxed while keeping the back straight.

As when learning tandem waterskiing, we should start slowly in slalom skiing, standing and staying inside the wake for a while. Inside the wake, we should move back and forth across the turbulence zone. This drill is intended to teach balance and control. The difference between two-ski turning and one-ski turning is that there is no turn-to ski from which pressure is removed to initiate the turning motion, so we must learn to control our body's vertical angle to cause the ski to be angled relative to the water's surface. The body angle causes the slalom ski's turning motion. The best way to learn how to control our position in the wake is to practice. Later, after we have some experience, we will take a more theoretical view of the interaction of forces among the water, the waterski, and the waterskier.

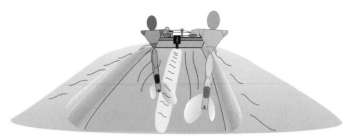

Figure 214. Practice moving inside wake

By the end of the turbulence zone crossing drill, a skier will likely tired, so let's perform a **slalom skiing release**, which is nothing more than giving the spotter the usual "release" signal and letting go of the tow line handle. The slalom skiing release can be fun because, unlike the tandem skiing release, the Slalom Skier has the option of making a quick cut to spin before completely sinking. Once in the water, good Slalom Skiers always give the spotter the "Okay" arm signal.

Figure 215. Slalom ski release

Let's now learn how to perform a **slalom ski deep water start** so that we can forego having to drop a ski, which requires the driver to pick up the ski at the end of our run or having to get the ski to allow us to start slalom skiing again. A slalom ski deep water start is similar to a tandem ski start in some ways but different in others. The similarities are in the bent arms, bent knee(s), straight back, ski straight up with ski tip high out of the water, and sitting position. The differences are that the single ski requires faster speed to begin planing, so we will find that we must hold the handle tighter, will be dragged through the water longer, need to be more patient while allowing the boat to get to speed, will have water up in the face, and have to control the position of the ski beneath us much more than when getting up on two skis.

There are two approaches that may be used during a deep water slalom ski start. The first approach is to have both feet in their respective slalom boots. The second approach is to put the front foot in the front boot but to allow the rear leg to drag behind. This second method allows us to lean forward over the ski during the start to help get the ski to plane faster. The second method is used by people who find the boat acceleration with themselves being towed behind causes them to drag behind the boat an excessive amount of time. On the other hand, keeping both feet in the ski is may be preferred because both legs can be used to keep the ski straight and absorb the force of the ski pushing up-ward. No matter which approach is used, a skier should always *take the opportunity* to position him or herself to be comfortable.

Figure 216. Tip up

Figure 217. Take up slack

We see here that Gary is using the two feet in boots slalom ski deep water start. Notice that he maintains his seated-in-a-chair position, holds the tow line to the inside of the front leg, keeps knees bent and toward his chest, positions the ski tip high out of the water and directly between him and the boat. As the water creeps up into his face and eyes, Gary holds his breath and closes his eyes, if necessary. The main focus is maintaining ones's balance and keeping that ski tip above the surface of the water to allow the ski to get planing as soon as possible.

Figure 218. Head high

Figure 219. Hold on tight

Once the boat gets to a speed sufficient to allow the ski to support this weight of the skier, Gary will slowly straighten up from that bent knee sitting position to a slightly bent knee, straight hips and back position. Finally, when the boat gets to full speed, the ski will plane on the water and Gary will be able to stand comfortably near-vertical, just as when dropping a ski.

Figure 220. Keep ski straight

Figure 221. Balance

Figure 222. Hold position

Figure 223. Relax and ski

As a practical matter, the deep water slalom start should take anywhere from five to twenty-five seconds, depending on the acceleration of the boat, the weight of the skier, and the skier's effort to lean over the ski to get the ski to plane more quickly. If the angle of the ski turns sideways or the ski tip dips beneath the water's surface, the skier should immediately release the tow line so as not to expend energy on a futile start attempt. Most Slalom Skiers take between three and nine attempts at their first deep water start. After ten attempts, the skier should either be given the second tandem ski or be brought back into the boat for a rest because performing a deep water start takes considerable energy and endurance. After successfully completing a slalom deep water start, we, as Slalom Skiers, should continue practicing, to make deep water slalom starts as natural as our tandem ski deep water starts have become.

Figure 224. Both feet in boots   *Figure 225. Drag right leg at start*

The first set of exercises Slalom Skiers should practice is **crossing a wake crest**. At the beginning, Slalom Skiers can lean in the direction they wish to move. The amount of force the skier should exert backward, to prevent simply falling sideways while leaning into the turn, should be commensurate with the sharpness of the turn. So, during the first drill where we would like to get comfortable and familiar with moving out of and back into the wake, the force is very little. This allows us to concentrate on keeping our weight evenly distributed on the ski.

Figure 226. Distribute weight on ski

The next exercise we should work on is maintaining control over our position behind the boat while the boat is turning. Slalom Skiers can stay in the wake, move to the outside of the wake and turn, or try to stay outside the wake but on the inside of the turn. Practicing turns on the inside of the wake will give Slalom Skiers the ability to handle situations in which the driver inadvertently begins to turn while the skier is skiing on the turn-to side of the wake.

Figure 227. Control position in wake around turn

Slalom Skiers will come to find that, when **crossing waves**, the single ski provides more stability than when skiing on two skis. One ski, supporting all of a skier's weight, will cut through the waves. In addition, having both feet in boots along the length of the ski will control the angle of the ski such that it does not slide beneath us as tandem skis tended to do. Just as we do when tandem skiing, however, we should bend our knees to absorb shocks when crossing waves and to lower our center of gravity to add stability.

Figure 228. Hold cut through wake

Now that we've learned the deep water start, understand how to move left and right, can control our position while the boat turns, let's get more aggressive with our turns and begin to cross from one side of the wake to the other. The first skill we must improve to help make the cut easier and more coordinated is the slalom hand position on the handle. The **slalom hand position** in this context means palm up or palm down, where palm up would indicate the palm is facing the sky, and palm down indicates the palm is facing toward the water. Many Slalom Skiers hold the handle during the cut such that the inside hand is palm up. The outside hand will hold the handle palm down (some skiers hold the handle with palms reversed, inside down and outside up). For example, if the skier were cutting from starboard to port (i.e., skier's right to left), the left hand would be the inside hand, and, therefore, the left hand palm would be facing the sky during the cut while holding the handle.

Figure 229. Hand releasing practice

The next part of **slalom hand coordination** during a cut is placing the hands along the handle. The inside hand with palm up should hold the handle to the inside of the turn to allow room for the palm down hand to get a firm grip. For those who find holding the handle vertically is more comfortable during the cut, the palm up hand would be holding the handle toward the top, and the palm down hand would then have gripping room at the bottom. Note that the palm up hand's palm naturally faces the other hand when the handle is held in the vertical position. Hand position and placement along the handle may seem too complicated to remember while slalom skiing, especially in the early stages of learning, but, with a little practice, shifting hands in preparation for the next cut will become very natural. The goal here is to get us to start thinking about body position, which includes coordinating all body parts, including the hands.

This brings us to the **slalom arm coordination**, which are the reason for having learned about hand position. The arms perform the function of pulling the handle toward the body, specifically toward the outside hip, to keep the tow line taut during the entire cut. As we begin to take sharper cuts while slalom skiing, we will find that the tow line will begin to slacken as we turn toward the boat with slight forward momentum. The line becomes taut again once turned toward the wake. The short period in which a skier faces the boat, however, is a potential for line-slack, causing a moment of unbalance, since there is no force opposing the skier's lean. Note that the Slalom Skier's lean is inward, diagonally toward the boat at that moment. To keep the line taut so as not to experience unbalance while facing the boat, the skier's arms should pull the handle toward the outside hip, as suggested. Pulling the handle toward the hips (as opposed to the shoulders) keeps the center of effort (pull of the tow line) low, which helps the skier maintain balance. And, pulling toward the outside hip rather than inside hip will increase the turning force to help get the body and ski angled quickly toward the wake. Note that the ability to comfortably pull the handle across the body to the outside hip begins with holding the handle with one palm up and one palm down.

Figure 230. Pull handle to outside hip, inside palm up

125

As suggested, a good cut is made by having the total body coordinated toward that goal, so let's look at the next contributor, the eyes. The eyes play a big role in making a sharp cut because the body tends to follow the direction the eyes are looking, which, in

Figure 231. Look across wake during cut

this case, should be across the wake. The head, of course, will turn to face the opposite side of the wake, then the turn will be completed when the body and ski follow. The hand and arm motions have become instinctive and coordinated through practice by this point, so we can concentrate on looking across the wake. Likewise, we have crossed the wake many times, so we should not find ourselves looking down at our ski.

Before adding other body parts, let's take a minute to put what we have covered so far together with crossing the wake from port to starboard then back to port. First, note that the action was to cross from "port to starboard then back to port" rather than "from port to starboard" only or "from port to starboard then from starboard to port." The reason for not stopping or delaying in crossing back to the first side is to get us in the frame of mind, and to practice the technique, of making continuous turning motions. Stopping or delaying, especially while trying to learn and improve, will form bad habits. We want (and need) to make continuous cuts from one side to another to make the kind of improvements necessary to allow these drills to be successful. So, when crossing from port

Figure 232. More aggressive cut

Figure 233. Continue to practice both sides

to starboard, we are getting our hands into position for making the next cut. This hand motion usually occurs immediately after crossing the second wake crest, which is the starboard wake crest in this situation. The hand shift can be made quickly by simply releasing the to-be outside hand from the handle and rotating the handle to make the palm down hand now palm up. The now palm up hand could, in fact, maintain grip in the center of the handle, leaving room for the other hand to grip on the outside or lower part of the handle, depending on one's handle positioning style. Once across the starboard wake, the skier should immediately think of cutting back to port. The first move (in what we have discussed) is to look back across to port, pulling the tow line handle to the outside hip (right hip, when on starboard), and holding that position until across the wake where the corresponding port-to-starboard hand, head, and arm motions will be performed to cut back to starboard.

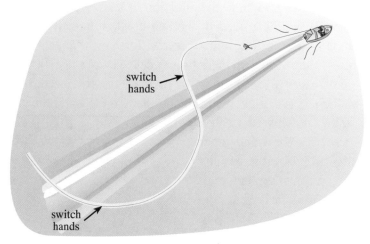

Figure 234. Timing hand switch during slalom skiing

At this point, our goals should be to successfully cross the wake, make the proper hand transfers, and convince our eyes to stay focused back across the wake while turning. The cuts need not look like Gary and Mark's, which are tight for illustrative purposes. Practicing going back and forth from port to starboard to port to starboard several times, and using the hand, eyes, and arms in synchronization is all one should be concerned with for now, not the amount of water being thrown or the tightness of the turn.

Let's take detailed look at the **slalom skiing forces** involved in a slalom ski turn. In waterskiing, with every action, there is an equal and opposite reaction; when there is not, we fall. When the slalom skier leans, the ski will exert a horizontal force along the surface of the water away from the turning direction. At the same time, the ski will be

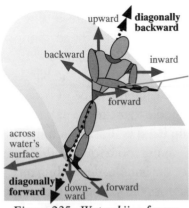

Figure 235. Waterskiing forces

angled away from the direction of the boat's forward path, so, as a result, there will be a force along the surface of the water toward the boat. Adding up these two forces, we get a resultant force diagonally forward, away from the turning direction. The two counteracting forces are created by a skier's body motion and angle. The skier's lean sideways creates a force in the direction of lean. The skier's lean backward (beyond the normal standing-up-straight lean backward that keeps tension on the tow line) creates a force in the direction away from the boat. Adding up these two forces, we get a resultant force diagonally away from the boat in the direction of the turn. To complete this discussion, the resultant force on the water due to the

ski is angled downward because of our body weight and other downward forces on the ski. The upward forces on the body result from the restorative forces of the water pushing back on the ski. Combining all these forces, we have a large force angled diagonally forward and downward into the water, counteracted by a large force angled diagonally backward and upward. The net result is an equal and opposite reaction, so the skier will successfully complete the turn. This

Figure 236. Look across wake

Figure 237. Keep hips high

basic analysis neglects effects from other forces, such as drag or the forces created by traveling across the wake then making the turn. But, by simple extension, when skiing across the wake into a cut, the force vector outward (away from the turn) would be increased during the turn, then angled forward at the end of the turn, so leaning into the turn and away from the boat can be increased. This discussion helps explain why skiers making very sharp turns are able to angle themselves so close to the water. This theoretical discussion is intended to help us understand what is happening among the ski, water, and waterskier, but only practice and experience will make us able to waterski better. The rest of the Slalom Skills section is dedicated to practical waterskiing exercises.

Now that we have a more theoretical understanding of the interactions among the ski, water, tow line pull, and body lean, let's add hip, leg, and foot positions to our hand, arm, and eye coordination while making a cut. While making a cut, the slalom skier's hips should be kept as though standing upright in as natural a position as possible. If severe bending occurs at the waist, the torso will be too far forward, placing one's center of gravity in front of the fore ski boot, making turns difficult to initiate and causing excess leg effort to make the slalom ski turn in the direction desired. If a slalom skier finds him or herself bending excessively at the waist, he or she will have to concentrate on keeping the body straight from shoulder to foot (or even think about pushing the hips forward) until weight becomes evenly balanced over the two feet during a cut.

Figure 238. Keep hips forward, legs and back straight, look across wake

The **slalom leg position** provide the support for the skier during the cut. The strongest support will be made by keeping the knees virtually straight during the cut. One can imagine the downward force of the torso transmitting through the legs onto the ski, then the upward force of the water on the ski transmitting back up the legs to the torso. If the knees are bent, the leg muscles will be required to withstand the body weight during each cut, which can be exhausting on the leg muscles. Keeping the legs straight will reduce muscle exertion. Likewise, keeping the legs in line with the torso rather than sweeping the ski out to the side during a cut will have the same effect on other leg muscles.

The last body position we will be concerned with is the **slalom feet position**. The feet should be kept flat against the ski to keep the ski firmly beneath the skier. A boot that does not properly fit will allow the ski to rotate slightly or force the foot into having to work to stay flat against the ski. A foot doing extra work may cramp during, or ache after, a long run. Soft padding beneath the foot, and a well-fitted boot, can make waterskiing more comfortable and can also provide the skier with the sure-footedness required to improve his or her cutting ability.

At this point, we have covered the details that help to make a good cut, so we are ready to consider **how to throw water** high and full. From the theoretical discussion, we learned that speed going into a cut will enable the skier to lean lower during the cut. The junction where the ski and water's surface meet defines how much water will be part of the spray, sometimes referred to as a rooster tail because of its shape. The more angled the ski from planing on the water and the

Figure 239. Think about each element of the cut

Figure 240. Make cut more aggressive

130

Figure 241. Keep body straight

Figure 242. Maintain speed and position

faster the ski contacts the water, the more water that will be lifted into the air. Keeping in mind that the body is kept straight and the feet remain flat on the ski, one sees that the amount of water thrown is directly proportional to how low one can get to the water (omitting other factors, such as a skier's weight, the shape of the ski, and fin holes). To support the body angle, the slalom skier must cross the wake aggressively to build speed for the cut or lean outward (as if to ski wide) then use this speed to lean low during the cut.

While **making a tight cut**, we should hold the cut all the way into and across the wake by using the hand, arm, and eye techniques discussed earlier. Lifting out of the lean prior to hitting the wake will disrupt the smooth spray we are trying to maintain through the cut. Remember, a constant pulling force by the tow line (augmented by pulling the handle toward the outside hip) will allow a constant lean angle into and through the wake.

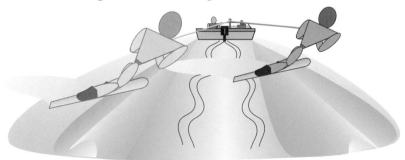

Figure 243. Hold cut position across wake

A **slalom waterskiing course** can be set up to help improve our cutting speed and style. A slalom course consists of a driving lane, through which the motorboat will travel, and skier turning buoys, to the outside of which the skier must pass. The driving lane and skier turning points are defined by buoys, which are relatively inexpensive and easy to assemble by simply using inexpensive buoys attached by inexpensive line, such as cotton or thin nylon line, to water jugs filled with sand. The skier's buoys should be spaced along the length of the lane to challenge skiers to go around two successive buoys; the driving lane buoys should be placed so the skier is away from the driving lane buoys when crossing to the next skier buoy. The distance the buoys are placed from the center of the driving lane will also make passing to the outside of successive buoys challenging, and the farther away from the driving lane the buoys are set, the more the skier will be challenged. When a skier learns to pass easily around all the course buoys, the tow line should be shortened to increase the difficulty for the skier. A shorter forces the skier to make tighter turns to accelerate across the wake to get to the next buoy in time to ski around it.

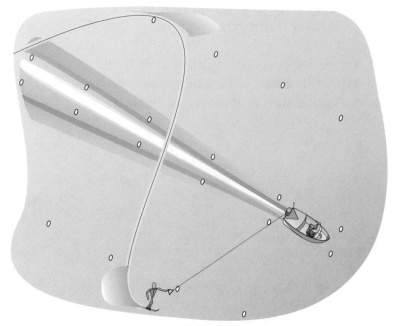

Figure 244. Slalom buoy course

The last slalom skiing skill we will be learning is the **whip cut**, also known as a French cut. The whip cut is performed during a boat turn, or preferably a whip (extremely tight boat turn) whereby the skier skis to the outside of the turn to gain speed and uses the additional speed to increase the amount of water that will be thrown. The additional speed will enable the skier to extend the length of the turn and lower the skier's angle with respect to the water, producing some enormous, smooth, beautiful sprays. Also, because the boat is turning, it has less forward speed, so the skier will tend to sink slightly during the tail end of the whip cut, causing even more water than usual to be contacted and thrown by the ski!

Figure 245. Starting whip-cut

Figure 246. Whip-cut goes slow and low

Figure 247. Hold same position when crossing wake

Remember, total body coordination will make cutting easier and will increase the length of our runs. Everything we have learned about waterskiing is employed during all phases of a slalom skiing run to make our day on the water safe, fun, and exciting!

Congratulations on your efforts...

**...and thank you for joining us while
WATERSKIING and Getting off the Ground with you!**

Slalom Review

1. **Tow Line Inspection**. We learned to replace lines should they become frayed, particularly a tow line and tow line bridle. What causes wear and fraying to the tow line and tow line bridle, which are made of polypropylene line?

2. **Anchor Lines and Dock Lines**. (a) An eyesplice will make a (temporary / permanent) loop at the end of a line? (choose the correct answer). (b) Shackles should be used to connect the anchor chain to the thimble spliced into the anchor rode (line) to prevent the line from _____ where the metal might otherwise contact the line?

3. **Waterski Performance**. Name a benefit of a short and a long waterski.

4. **Stretching**. Write a list of muscles that slalom skiers should stretch before slalom waterskiing (and tandem waterskiing).

5. **Dropping a Ski**. A slalom waterskier dropping a ski should loosen the boot on the ski to be dropped, and the driver should slow the motorboat to give the waterskier more stability while performing the drop. What are the steps recommended for the slalom skier to actually release the ski?

6. **Deep Water Slalom Start**. (a) What is one advantage to starting with both feet in their respective boots during a deep water slalom start? (b) What is one advantage to starting with one leg dragging behind during a deep water slalom start?

7. **Hand and Arm Position**. When making a cut, the slalom skier turns the (outside / inside) hand palm up or down to pull the tow line handle to the (outside / inside) hip to keep sufficient tension on the tow line to make a strong cut. (choose the correct choices).

8. **Eye/Body Coordination**. To help the body make a good cut, the slalom skier should look across the wake through the cut and continue looking across the wake while crossing through the wake.

9. **Waterskiing Theory**. In waterskiing, with every action, there is an equal and opposite reaction; when there is not, we _____.

10. **Whip Cut**. A whip cut provides a skier with an opportunity to... (fill in the rest of the sentence).

Bonus:

Teach others the sport of waterskiing to re-enforce the knowledge you have gained from "WATERSKIING - Getting off the Ground!"

Index

Beginner Answers

1. **PFD Types**. A Type II PFD is often orange in color and horseshoe shaped, requiring the wearer to tie straps near the neck and to clip a strap around the waist. The Type II PFD is intended to keep the wearer's breathing passages out of the water should the wearer be floating while unconscious. A Type III PFD is a vest-style PFD that provides the wearer with more freedom of movement than does the Type II PFD, making the Type III PFD applicable for use in waterskiing. (see page 11).

2. **Recommended Safety Equipment**. (a) audible/visible signals, first aid kit, spare PFD, extra line, spare paddle, anchor, backboard, fire extinguisher, lights, sunglasses, shoes with nonskid soles. (b) cellular phone, mask, snorkel and fins, tool kit. (see pages 14-15).

3. **Boat Nomenclature**. (a) General: bow, stern, port (left), starboard. (b) Specific: Cockpit, deck, seats, steering wheel, engine, gunnels, transom, hull, windshield, lights, battery, horn. (see pages 16-17).

4. **Waterski Nomenclature**. Tip, edge, fin, boot, slalom boot. (see page 17).

5. **Pre-ski Audible Signals**. (a) "Wait!" - do not accelerate. "Hit it!" - accelerate the boat. "Take up the slack!" - put the boat into forward to pull the tow line until it is in tension (straight) between the skier and the boat. (b) "No!" and "Go!" because they sound so similar. (see pages 24-25).

6. **Skier Hand Signals and Spotter Arm Signals**. (a) The skier gives a "thumbs-up" signal to tell the driver to speed up the motorboat, a "thumbs-down" signal to slow the boat, an "Okay" signal when the speed is comfortable, and a "slash across the throat" to indicate "releasing the handle". (see pages 25-26).

7. **Fallen Skier Arm Signals**. (a) One arm means, "I need help or I wish to enter the boat." (b) Two arms forming and "O" means, "I'm Okay." (c) No raised arms means, "I need immediate assistance!" (see pages 27-28).

8. **Skier's Stance**. (a) The waterskis are kept parallel to each other with tips high out of the water and between the skier and boat when the skier is performing a deep water start. (b) The waterskis should be kept parallel to each other approximately shoulder-width apart while waterskiing. (see pages 35-39).

9. **Parts of the Motorboat Wake**. Turbulence zone, port/starboard crest, port/starboard trough. (see pages 39).

10. **Moving Left and Right Inside the Wake**. To move left, the skier should take pressure off the <u>left</u> ski. Similarly, to move right, the skier should take pressure off the <u>right</u> ski. (see page 40).

Advanced Answers

1. **Wetsuit**. A snug-fitting wetsuit is a good insulator. So, when a thin film of water fills the wetsuit and is held against the waterskier's body, the thin film of cold water warms to body temperature and, consequently, keeps the skier warm. (see page 46).

2. **Tow line**. (a) When bringing the line into the boat, we can simply allow the line to fall randomly into a small area. This random distribution will rarely cause a tangle or knot. (b) The tow line handle should be placed <u>away</u> from the tow line to prevent a knot from being formed. (see page 50).

3. **Driver/Spotter/Skier Responsibilities**. While pre-ski scouting the water-way, we should look for natural and man-made objects. Natural objects found on or in a waterway include: logs, rocks, branches, shallow water, and weeds - usually found near the shoreline. Man-made objects to avoid are docks, rafts, moored boats, moving boats, swimmers, other waterskiers, and other objects that could impede a boat or skier's forward travel. (see page 51).

4. **Overboard Person**. Equipment available on a boat to extend to an overboard person or drowning victim in the water are waterskis, PFD's, spare paddle, tow line, towel, shirt, spare line, seat cushion, or arm. Remember, never enter the water, even if trained in lifeguard rescue techniques, unless absolutely necessary. (see page 52).

5. **Injured Skier**. Once safely on a backboard, the victim's head and neck should be immobilized. No head movement or neck twisting should be done outside the supervision of a trained medical emergency specialist. Medical help should be sought as soon as possible for this or any other waterskier injury. (see pages 52-53).

6. **Crossing a Wake Crest**. To help an inexperienced waterskier cross a wake crest, some tips might be: to be assertive, angle the ski tips toward the wake crest to be crossed, bend the knees, keep feet shoulder width apart, and stay balanced. (see pages 54-58).

7. **Crossing Waves**. The larger the waves to be crossed, the more we should bend our knees. The rest of the body should remain relaxed. The arms should bend as required to take up tow line slack. (see page 59).

8. **Dock Start**. (a) Three spread-arm lengths of line should be the first length used when attempting a dock start. (b) If a skier sinks into the water after coming off the dock, he or she should <u>increase</u> the length of line placed into the water, (e.g., try four spread-arm lengths), to allow the boat to gain more speed before beginning to pull the skier. (see page 64).

9. **Skier Salute**. The <u>tip</u> of the ski should be angled upward to prevent it from contacting the water and being pulled off while performing the skier's salute. (see pages 65-66).

10. **Kneeboarding**. To keep the leading edge angled upward to prevent the water from climbing over the leading edge, which will cause the kneeboard rider to tumble forward, the kneeboard rider always leans away from the direction of travel. (see pages 67-71).

Driver Answers

1. **Boat Anchors**. A mushroom anchor, so named because of its mushroom-like shape, likes muddy waterway bottoms to use suction force to help it stay put. Danforth anchors have spades that dig into sand, mud, or wedge beneath rocks and should be equipped with a trip line. (see pages 74-75).

2. **Fire Extinguisher**. Water will spread the burning oil and gas, thereby spreading the fire. Since oil and gas float on water, chemical and Halon gas fire extinguishers should be used because they provide a safe and efficient means for putting out an oil and gas fire. (see page 75).

3. **Electrical Equipment**. All electrical equipment, including the lights, horn, bilge pump, and radio require energy. The battery has a limited amount of energy before it needs a recharge, just like a car battery. Use of electrical equipment should be minimized between boat uses. (see pages 76-78).

4. **Fuel Storage**. When storing gasoline and oil, careful Drivers keep these chemicals in a cool, locked, ventilated shed. The liquids should be held in leak-free containers. No matches for other burning instruments should be used in or around such a storage area. (see page 81).

5. **Fuel Handling**. (a) Wash the eye from the tear duct outward for several minutes with water to clear the gasoline, then seek medical attention. (b) If someone ingests gasoline, that person should be taken for medical attention immediately! (see page 81).

6. **Fuel line**. Sand that gets into the fuel or fuel line has the potential to work its way into the engine. Although most engines have fuel filters, a piece of sand may get into the engine and cause irreparable damage to the engine's cylinders. (see pages 81-83).

7. **Starting the Engine**. On cold days, a Driver may need to either choke the engine or raise the idle speed or both. After the engine starts, the choke should be set to no-choke position and the idle should slowly be brought down to the slowest setting. (see pages 87-88).

8. **Driving in Forward and Reverse**. (a) The bow turns toward port when driving in forward and turning the steering wheel toward port. (b) The bow turns toward starboard when driving in reverse and turning the steering wheel to port. The best way to remember the bow motion with respect to the steering wheel motion is to go do it. (see pages 89-91).

9. **Driving for a Skier**. (a) Some Driver duties and tips to get the tow line to a skier preparing to perform a deep water start are: always maintain eye contact with the skier, circle the skier on the driver's side then head into the wind or water current (whichever is stronger), drive no faster than necessary. (b) The Driver can use the full throttle acceleration and smooth acceleration (drag) methods to pull up a skier. (see pages 99-103).

10. **Pulling a Skier**. Before turning to port, a Driver should check that the skier is in the wake or on the starboard side of the wake. Before turning to starboard, the Driver should check that the skier is in the wake or on the port side of the wake. The check should be conducted by asking the spotter. (see page 104).

Slalom Answers

1. **Tow Line Inspection**. Polypropylene wears through contact with sand and debris that gets into the line, causing microcuts into the polypropylene strands that leads to line fraying. Care should also be taken to keep people from stepping on the line. The sun and general weathering will also contribute to tow line and tow line bridle decay. (see pages 106-107).

2. **Anchor Lines and Dock Lines**. (a) An eyesplice will make a <u>permanent</u> loop at the end of a line. (b) The thimble spliced into an anchor line is intended to prevent metal from <u>wearing</u> the line. The thimble will not move relative to the line, so no line wear will occur. (see pages 107-110).

3. **Waterski Performance**. In general, a shorter waterski will allow the skier to take tighter turns than longer skis. A longer waterski tends to be more stable than shorter waterskis. (see pages 112-113).

4. **Stretching**. Slalom waterskiers should stretch all of their body muscles, particularly the calves, hamstrings, and quadriceps. The neck and shoulders are also important areas to stretch before waterskiing. (see page 115).

5. **Dropping a Ski**. The steps recommended for releasing the waterski are: (1) lift the heel of the foot; (2) lift the ball of the foot out of the ski boot; (3) move the released foot to the slalom ski slalom boot strap; (4) insert the released foot into the slalom ski slalom boot strap. (see pages 116-118).

6. **Deep Water Slalom Start**. (a) One advantage to starting with two feet in boots is that both feet can be used to keep the ski pointed toward the boat with the tip high out of the water. (b) One advantage to starting with one foot dragging behind during a deep water start is that it allows the skier to lean forward, over the ski, to help the skier plane sooner. (see pages 119-122).

7. **Hand and Arm Position**. The <u>inside</u> hand is turned palm up (or down) to pull the tow line handle to the <u>outside</u> hip. (see pages 124-125).

8. **Eye/Body Coordination**. True. The body will tend to move in the direction the eyes are looking. Looking down at the skis or wake or looking at the boat will tend to reduce one's turning coordination and speed across the wake, plus it is always a good idea to watch where you are going. (see pages 126-127).

9. **Waterskiing Theory**. <u>Fall</u>. If there is no counter force to the turn, a skier will fall. The easiest example to the equal and opposite force is the one that supports a skier on the water. Water passing beneath the ski traveling across it is sufficient to keep the skier standing. When making a cut, there are just more forces involved that support the skier's angle during the cut. (see page 128-129).

10. **Whip Cut**. ...ski fast and throw a lot of water, which can be described as an enormous, beautiful spray. (see pages 133-134).

Robert Tannenbaum
B&W Photography

Amy Lynn
Contributing B&W Photography
Front Cover (bottom) Photograph
Back Cover Photography

Alex Sherman - Front Cover Pyramid Top

"Sailing's a Breeze!" and *"Paddle to Perfection!"* are part of the Aquatics Unlimited *"Getting off the Ground!"* instructional watersport series. Both instructional boating courses are available in book, video, and water-safe quick reference guide formats. The videos are professionally produced, and the author-illustrated, photo-packed books provide students with questions and answers to measure learning progress. Great for beginners, intermediates, and those teaching others. SAB! and PTP! are book and video shelf musts! *"Waterskiing - Getting off the Ground!"* and *"The Kayak Express!"* are available in book format and offer the same quality and instruction.

Sailing's a Breeze! 3-piece set　　*Paddle to Perfection! 3-piece set*

Beginner

- ☐ safety
- ☐ use of PFD
- ☐ safety equipment
- ☐ nomenclature
- ☐ swimming skills
- ☐ boarding/deboarding
- ☐ skier signals
- ☐ entering the water
- ☐ re-entering the boat
- ☐ putting on skis
- ☐ swimming with skis
- ☐ tandem deep water start
- ☐ tandem skiing
- ☐ parts of the wake
- ☐ tandem run release

Advanced

- ☐ waterskiing equipment
- ☐ knots
- ☐ tossing the line
- ☐ coiling the line
- ☐ responsibilities
- ☐ person overboard
- ☐ down skier rescue
- ☐ artificial respiration
- ☐ leaving the wake
- ☐ entering the wake
- ☐ crossing the wake
- ☐ waterskiing drills
- ☐ dock start
- ☐ skier salute
- ☐ kneeboarding

Driver

- ☐ boat equipment
- ☐ propeller types
- ☐ boat hauling
- ☐ dealing with fuel
- ☐ starting the engine
- ☐ disembarking
- ☐ scouting the water
- ☐ rules of the road
- ☐ trimming the boat
- ☐ gravity/buoyancy
- ☐ docking and beaching
- ☐ driving
- ☐ getting line to skier
- ☐ pulling up a skier
- ☐ driving with a skier
- ☐ returning for a skier

Slalom

- ☐ line types
- ☐ caring for line
- ☐ tying an eyesplice
- ☐ whipping
- ☐ making an anchor
- ☐ tossing a heaving line
- ☐ selecting waterskis
- ☐ tow line types
- ☐ waterski boom
- ☐ dropping a ski
- ☐ slalom deep water start
- ☐ slalom skiing stance
- ☐ leaving the wake
- ☐ cutting
- ☐ arm/hand coordination
- ☐ throwing a spray (rooster tails)